To, LAMA NORBU

[handwritten inscription in Tibetan script]

the backdoor to enlightenment

[handwritten inscription in Tibetan script]

[handwritten inscription in Tibetan script]

La Rinpoche

2008

the Backdoor to enlightenment

SHORTCUTS TO HAPPINESS FOR THE SPIRITUALLY CHALLENGED

za Rinpoche
and Ashley Nebelsieck

THREE LEAVES PRESS

DOUBLEDAY | NEW YORK

THREE
LEAVES
PRESS

PUBLISHED BY THREE LEAVES PRESS

Copyright © 2007 Zachoeje Rinpoche Lama and Ashley
Nebelsieck

All Rights Reserved

Published in the United States by Three Leaves Press, an imprint
of The Doubleday Broadway Publishing Group, a division of Random House, Inc., New York.

www.doubleday.com

Three Leaves Press and its colophon are trademarks of
Random House, Inc.

LIBRARY OF CONGRESS CATALOGING-IN-PUBLICATION DATA
Rinpoche, Za.
    The Backdoor to enlightenment : shortcuts to happiness for the
spiritually challenged / by Za Rinpoche and Ashley Nebelsieck.
        p. cm.
1. Buddhism—Doctrines. 2. Enlightenment (Buddhism)
I. Nebelsieck, Ashley. II. Title.

BQ4132.Z3 2007
294.3'44—dc22
2007023169

ISBN 978-0-7679-2740-6

PRINTED IN THE UNITED STATES OF AMERICA

10 9 8 7 6 5 4 3 2 1

FIRST EDITION

contents

The Backdoor to Enlightenment

As you go the way of life, you will see a great chasm.
Jump. It is not as wide as you think.

—NATIVE AMERICAN ADVICE

INTRODUCTION | enlightenment NOW

"Achieve what was never lost," Otto Mackenzie read
the sign above the massive door. He had worked at
the Philosophical Study Center Library for years
now, but only just noticed these faded words
carved into the stone lintel. "I will," Otto promised the sign as he juggled a stack of lecture bulletins in his long arms. "Just as soon as I achieve all
this work that I'm supposed to have finished by
three." He looked at his watch; it was five-thirty.
He closed his blue eyes, opened the door, and
took a deep breath through his prominent nose.

It was this smell, he decided, that kept him
here, despite all the hassles with the director and
his wife. He was poorly paid, never praised, and
sometimes had to work weekends, but each time
he opened the door he was enveloped by what
Otto imagined was the saddest, most beautiful
aroma in all the world: thousands of centuries-old
books, ancient leather bindings and handmade

paper, slowly decaying on the shelves. The only light poured in from the skylight, illuminating dust as it floated and settled on the great oak study table in the center of the room.

"Emma?" Otto pronounced hesitatingly to the dim corners of the library, hoping that the lack of fluorescent lights and her closed office door meant that his boss had gone. She would be furious that he had missed his deadline—the bulletins would have to go out a day late—and even angrier that the new librarian had left early and forgotten to lock up. Before Otto could flick the lights on to look for the spare key hidden in the mahogany paneling, a rustling in the darkness startled him.

"Hello?" a small voice called out to him.

Otto walked up the spiral staircase to the second floor, where the young librarian sat at the foot of a tall glass bookcase. "It's Hannah, right?"

She pushed her long auburn hair away from her pleasant face and nodded. Clearly, she had been crying. Otto usually didn't have the patience for these types of displays, but seeing her sitting there so forlorn, he suddenly realized he was exhausted. He sat down beside her and slapped his stack of overdue bulletins onto the hardwood floor. "I thought you went home," he said to her.

"A librarian never abandons her post," she sniffed.

"Did something happen with Emma, that mean old cow?" Otto guessed.

Hannah nodded. "I think she sold the Dürer engravings I found in the attic last week to a private collector." She clutched the stack of books she had been re-shelving to her chest, apparently for strength.

"Well, the library must need the money," Otto said.

"That's what I figured when I gave her the illuminated manuscript I found behind the Francis Bacon books, so she could put it in the vault," Hannah said. "These books are supposed to be available to everyone. That's why Robert Drake opened this library."

"Well, who knows, if you hadn't come along, those books might never have been found."

"Maybe Robert Drake hid his treasures because he didn't want people to sell them off when he wasn't around anymore. Did that thought ever occur to you?" Hannah said.

"Yes it has, on more than one occasion," Otto said.

"I heard he disappeared right after the Wycombes came to 'assist' him, and now they're selling off his stuff?"

Otto smiled at her attempts at conspiracy theory. "I never got to meet him, but I think he was pretty old—he opened this place in the forties—and sick. The important thing now is to keep his library open. I know he would have wanted that. Okay?"

Hannah nodded vigorously and shook off what remained of her self-pity. Otto gave her a hand to her feet and, no longer blinded by her emotion, she thought about her muddled appearance in the presence of the young man. His average, freckly looks were boosted by a Scottish accent. That coupled with a quiet reserve gave him an air of authority and made him nearly attractive.

He took a few of the books from her hands. "It's after five. What do you say I help you put these stragglers away and we get out of this place?"

"Those go in cabinet thirty-two. Bottom shelf. Some guy's been in here researching the Freemasons. He's had me up and down these stairs all day. Nearly emptied these two cabinets."

Hannah slipped the key ring, jangling, from her wrist and opened the bottom of cabinet 32 for Otto and cabinet 33 beside it.

"Are those the bulletins you brought up?" Hannah asked, kneeling to replace the books in their proper homes.

Otto stared into the open cabinet for a second. The books didn't seem to be in any order. He was eager to be done with his task and on his way home, so he just quietly jammed the books in wherever he could fit them.

"Yeah. Well, if Emma hadn't ordered so many last-minute changes, they would have been done yesterday."

"That was my fault," Hannah admitted, having to apply an unusual amount of pressure to one thin volume to fit it into the crowded cabinet. "She asked me to look it over and I found some mistake—Oh!" To her surprise the book passed beyond the other books and disappeared into a dark place between the others. She sat back on her heels and peered into the cabinet, confused. It seemed to her that the book had dropped off into some other world, and then recovering she remembered where she was. She had probably stumbled onto another one of Drake's hiding places. Between the well-known ones and the ones she found daily, the whole building seemed to her riddled with them.

"What happened?" Otto asked.

"Nothing," she said, disappointed that her tone was not more convincing.

"Come on, what just happened?"

She studied his face and the openness she found there led her to do something she vowed only minutes earlier she'd never do again, to share the secrets of Robert Drake. "I think I found something, Otto."

When they finished removing all the books from the bottom cabinet of case 33, Otto pointed out how the back panel of the bookcase slid over and pivoted just enough to swallow the thin volume of Saint-Germain's *Trinosophia*. He gingerly fished out the old book and handed it to her.

"Is there anything else in there?" Hannah asked.

"I don't have a flashlight," Otto said, meaning to convey that he did not intend to stick his hand back into that dark hole. He moved aside in the way of an invitation to her to take her chances. She didn't hesitate and after a moment feeling around elbow-deep in the darkness she brought to light a thin old package carefully wrapped in brown paper. Across the front the words *The Backdoor to Enlightenment* were written in a neat hand. She handed it to Otto.

"If it's as old as it looks, we could damage it by opening it," he said. "But Emma will open it and if it's valuable she'll put it in the vault along with the Gutenberg and everything else we aren't allowed to see."

"Or she'll just sell it without telling anyone," Hannah said. "Either way, we'll never see what's inside."

"And you did find it," Otto rationalized. "The 'Backdoor to Enlightenment,' huh?"

"Open it," Hannah said. "And we'll give it to her in the morning."

Otto untied the old twine and folded back the outer wrappings. Inside were a few beautifully painted stacked panels about four inches wide and twenty inches long. The gold lettering on the black background was foreign, possibly Tibetan or Sanskrit, Hannah surmised from her education in art history. At the top of each were careful depictions of a nomad, a lotus, and, on the last one, a golden wheel.

"These are priceless," Hannah said. "I wish we could read them."

"Look," Otto pointed out, shuffling the discarded layers of the wrapping. Set in old type, there appeared to be a translation. "It's in English."

They sat together quietly in the darkening library and read a story that few had ever seen.

Long ago, a nomad wandering tired through the desert came upon a small oasis. Beneath a magnificent tree, a clean spring sparkled in the sunlight. A white lotus floated on the surface. Many times he dipped his hand into the seemingly bottomless waters and took a sip. It was the sweetest, most wonderful nectar he had ever tasted. Immediately he felt great relief. Without his thirst, he saw the world in a different light. He felt comfortable and satisfied, cool under the hot sun. This surely must be a sacred spring, the man thought.

This man was very generous, for his first thought was to share the spring with the rest of the world. He set off to tell some of his friends about his discovery. They listened with rapt interest about the clear spring and the beautiful lotus and then followed him back to it. Immediately upon seeing it, his friends agreed with the man's claim. "We believe you have found a most sacred secret spring."

"Taste it," the man said, offering them a cup.

"We can't drink that," they agreed.

"Why not?" the man asked. "It's delicious."

"We don't doubt it tastes delicious," one friend said, "but it is sacred."

"We should all step away from the sacred spring," another friend said, "so we don't pollute it."

"Good idea," they all agreed and simultaneously took a step back.

"You can't pollute it," the man said. "It is bottomless."

"What did it taste like?" one other friend asked.

"Why do you want me to describe it?" the man said, a little exasperated. "Just taste it yourself."

"We must purify ourselves first. But you just drank this sacred nectar without any hesitation. You must also be holy."

"No, I am just a man who, when thirsty, has the sense to drink. You are all free to do what you want to do. I am going to look for those who thirst and invite them to come and drink from the spring."

"Good," a friend said. "You go, and we will stay here and guard the secret."

Dismayed that his thirsty friends preferred guarding the water to drinking it, he went to find people without such odd tendencies. In the desert he soon met more thirsty people and told them what he had found. Some decided to follow him to the lotus spring. There they found a proper fence of sticks built in front of the spring. His friends were deep in contemplation.

"Our holy master has returned," they said.

"Don't listen to them," he told the newcomers. "Here's the reason you have come. Taste this," he said, and walked to the spring.

"Holy places must," one friend said, "always be approached from the north."

"And commoners must remove their shoes," another said. "We must strive to be humble before the sacred spring."

The newcomers were grateful for this important information. They rushed to take off their shoes and bowed.

Then one of the newcomers addressed the group: "To protect such a sacred place, shouldn't we use more than a flimsy fence of sticks?" They agreed to build a stone and mortar wall as soon as possible.

The nomad tried to avoid the group of spring worshipers, but each time he returned for a drink, more people had crowded around the oasis. There they performed intricate rituals and recited long incantations. Eventually they built both an enormous temple and another wall to protect the spring. A priestly guard marched before the great complex that stood where once there was only a small desert oasis.

Travelers with spiritual leanings made the nectar spring famous throughout the land. Its waters could heal all ailments, some said. Once you tasted it, you would live forever, others said. All agreed the spring brought peace and happiness to whomever drank from it. But none approached.

Staring at the mobs in wonder, the nomad would calmly walk past the crowds, the gate, the walls, the temples, and directly to the spring where he would sit in peace and drink his fill.

On his way back to the desert, the people who gathered around the temple would plead with him to share a word about how he reached the spring. "I just walked past all the barriers."

The people nodded. "This man truly knows the way," they said. They didn't understand his words, so legends were written about him.

Years passed, and holy men now drew maps and described how they imagined the maze of walls and barricades could be negotiated in order to reach the nomad's lotus spring within. The nomad had grown old. Right before he died, he repeated the truth he'd always maintained: "Taste the delicious water. Don't mind the walls and guards. They cannot keep you out."

Everyone agreed this must mean something quite profound, and they remained in reverent silence as the holiest of men died, taking the secret of the lotus spring with him.

But many years later, another came to unlock the secret. It was no longer water this man sought to ease the thirst in the world, but enlightenment to ease the suffering; and he found it. Much like the nomad in the desert, the people who came after him built barriers and obstacles around his discovery. Like the lotus spring in the desert, through the secrets of the Six Perfections, enlightenment also has a backdoor. These verses reveal the mysteries that have been hidden.

Otto turned the paper over but found nothing on the other side.

"That's it?" he said.

"Complete texts this old are hard to come by. On his travels, Drake must have bought just these few panels. They are still probably worth a fortune. There are tons of fragments just like this in the Art Annex. I've been cataloging them for weeks. None this old or beautiful though," Hannah said.

"I studied religion in college," Otto said. "But I've never heard this story. It must be Buddhist though. The Six Perfections are qualities they say we're supposed to perfect to achieve enlightenment—generosity, morality—I don't remember the whole list."

"The writing's Tibetan. I wasn't sure at first. But it is. See these dots between the words?"

"Wow. What if the text is true? What if these are instructions telling how to achieve enlightenment?" Otto said.

"Through the Six Perfections? Otto, you said everyone already knows what they are. How's that a secret?"

"There must be something everyone's missed. I'm no expert, but I've never heard of *The Backdoor to Enlightenment*. Could you imagine? To see the world the way Jesus, the Buddha, and so many spiritual masters have seen it?"

"Well, imagining is all you're going to get to do," Hannah said as she stacked the rest of the books back into cabinet 33. "Because we don't have the rest of the manuscript. And by this time tomorrow, it will be locked in the vault." To enforce this point, she locked the cabinets and stood up.

"Or sold," Otto reminded her.

"Or sold," Hannah repeated sadly as she gathered the panels up and tenderly rewrapped them.

"Give me a day." Otto just blurted it out before he even thought about it. He considered his statement as Hannah did, and continued, "We already know Drake liked to hide things. What if he hid the rest of the manuscript somewhere else? Unless you want to wait years until someone stumbles on it by accident, the only chance we have of finding it is to study the notes to his translation."

"That's assuming he ever *had* the rest of it," Hannah said. "What makes you think he did? Why would he split it up?"

"If there was anyone who learned the secret to enlightenment, it was Drake. He set up this whole library for the pursuit of wisdom. If he had this kind of secret, he would leave clues so others could find it. But it makes sense to split it up. If someone accidentally found this part, it would be useless without the secrets of the Six Perfections, and maybe vice versa. Just give me one day to look into it."

"One day?" Hannah said. She didn't know why she was

bargaining with this man. His excitement had infected her, and now she was just as curious and hopeful about finding the rest of the panels as he was.

"I promise," Otto said. "We won't be hurting anyone by waiting a day. I'll copy the translation and we'll store the panels in the Art Annex with the other fragile texts. They'll be safe."

"Okay," Hannah agreed.

Otto brought the package downstairs. He thought about how different everything would be once he found the missing panels. Some people gave their whole lives to achieve enlightenment. Otto imagined having the wisdom of the sages at such a young age. Dreams of his success flooded his mind as he copied the translation.

From the top of the stairs, Drake's portrait caught Hannah's eye. His blue eyes stared up at her from a pale face, his black hair swept back in waves. We will keep your secret for one more day, Hannah promised the portrait.

From that vantage point, she noticed case 33 directly above the portrait, and above that, nestled in a large niche, a statue of the Buddha gazed down at her peacefully. Through the skylight she saw the stars twinkling in the clear evening sky.

The backdoor to enlightenment, Hannah thought. Could such a thing actually exist?

ILLUMINATING ENLIGHTENMENT NOW

How do you think your life would be different if you were enlightened? Would all of your prayers be answered? Would you have everything you always wanted? Be perfectly happy? Would you understand the mysteries of the universe and unravel the secrets of life? Maybe if you were awakened you could end war and suffering. Maybe you would even help everyone else in the world become enlightened as well. Imagine the possibilities. What is keeping you from this most profound realization? If you figured out a secret backdoor to unlock your potential, live your dreams, and open your life to happiness and bliss, would you have the courage to use it? You hold in your hands now the key to that backdoor.

Every religion and philosophy seems to have a theory about how you can achieve perfection, happiness, and inner peace, who deserves it, and why. Whether enlightenment comes after this life or is attained by many lifetimes of hard work, we all know we could be happier, have greater understanding, and live a more balanced life. We might not agree about the exact definition of perfection, but we know that we are not it.

If we are optimistic, we tell ourselves that once upon a time an enlightened being lived somewhere like India or the Middle East or Utah, and maybe someday we might live the life of an awakened being ourselves if we try very hard. In fact, the one thing we can agree on is that if enlightenment does exist, it exists sometime in the future or in the past. Our minds have utterly banished enlightenment from the present tense. How did that happen?

There's something scary about seeking wisdom. What if we don't like what we find? Existence is so vast that we fear we might lose ourselves if we gaze at it too deeply. Maybe, out of modesty, we think of enlightenment as fundamentally out of our reach. We have faults and make mistakes; how can enlightenment be meant for common people like us? Out of deference to our spiritual leaders, we have placed their achievements and understanding on a pedestal we dare not approach, somehow forgetting that they set an example so that *others might follow*.

One of those spiritual leaders, Siddhartha Gautama, the Buddha, was not a god, a prophet, or a messiah, but rather a normal human, just like us, who, by his own efforts, became an enlightened being. *Buddha* is a Sanskrit word meaning "enlightened or awakened one." He was born twenty-five hundred years ago into the prosperous royal family of the Shakya clan in northern India.

When Siddhartha was born, an astrologer predicted that he would either be a great king or he would leave the palace life to become a spiritual seeker. Siddhartha's father did not want his precious son to leave the kingdom and so provided him with unimaginable wealth. The king surrounded Siddhartha with everything he desired and hid the harsh realities of life beyond the palace walls. However, like many who are blessed with luxury, Siddhartha grew dissatisfied and began to wonder if he was wasting his life.

Siddhartha snuck outside the palace to the surrounding city and there saw sickness, old age, and death. Shocked by the harsh realities of existence, he felt an urgency to seek the true meaning of life. At twenty-nine, Siddhartha made the bold decision to leave his pampered life to wander and become a truth seeker. He approached spiritual masters who were also searching for the ultimate truth. He tried many methods and even went to the extreme of denying himself all comforts in hopes that this would be the path to realizing enlightenment. He studied all the best spiritual texts of the time and still could not learn how to overcome suffering. All the religious authorities told him he'd have to wait many lifetimes to be happy, and that liberation from suffering was a state reserved for the gods. But that wasn't a good enough answer for him. And it isn't a good enough answer for us either.

After six years of learning all he could from the ascetic masters and their methods, he was convinced that it was futile to attempt to attain enlightenment by even the most radical physical measures. Siddhartha set out alone to seek enlightenment beyond the physical world using his own mind. In a small grove near the banks of the Niranjana River, beneath a bodhi tree in Bodh Gaya, he sat and vowed to let go of all struggles and expectations. Siddhartha sat in deep meditation as the true nature of reality was exposed to him layer after layer. When Venus rose over the eastern horizon, his understanding of the causes of suffering and the means to end them became unshakable; he reached enlightenment, the fully awakened state. All of the answers he had been seeking had revealed themselves, and he felt a deep realization of truth that he could not express in words; he just giggled.

When, years later, one of his disciples asked him why he had laughed, he explained that he had been searching so long for enlightenment and finally realized he had been there all along. After all of his efforts, trials, and pains, he could see that the journey from the world of suffering to the world of enlightenment was just a shift in his understanding. Outwardly he was the same person, but he saw the world in a different light.

In his meditation, he identified the six qualities that made up his perfect state of equilibrium and happiness: generosity, morality, patience, effort, concentration, and wisdom—the Six Perfections. More than two thousand years later, every day, millions of people still pray that by perfecting these qualities they will become enlightened in order to help all other sentient beings to be happy and free from suffering.

Over the years, many scholars have analyzed the Path of Perfection and proposed different ways to achieve freedom from suffering. But after all their hard work, what-ever method was chosen the best-case scenario was that we could only hope to live in bliss after striving over *thou-sands* of lifetimes. Even to the most patient person, that might seem like an awfully long time to wait for happi-ness. And what if we aren't patient, or cannot say for cer-tain whether we have one lifetime or one billion ahead of us? Even if we believe in a life in heaven after death, it would still be nice to be happier now while we're alive. What the scholars always seem to overlook is that the Buddha also wanted to live in peace and be free from suf-fering *now*.

The Six Perfections were not traits Buddha adopted or worked to develop; they existed within him all along. *They are innate characteristics that we all possess.* The Buddha's re-alization was recognizing the qualities and the critical part they played in his enlightenment. In Tibetan, the word *perfection* literally translates as "crossing over to the other side," "gone beyond," or "balance." When the Buddha fully perceived the way these qualities permeated his very existence, he mentally crossed over from the world of suffering into that of enlightenment. He had "gone be-yond" the limitations of the physical world, beyond the idea of good and evil, to reach a perfect balance—perfect equilibrium. This book is designed to help you to go be-yond your limitations and cross into the world of peace and enlightened realization by recognizing how these same qualities already exist within you.

The Buddha recognized the Six Perfections as planks on a natural bridge that we could use to cross the sea of suffering into a state of enlightenment, but we have taken this bridge and created rules around it, turning each step into another impassable barrier. Instead of appreciating the ultimate nature of these qualities, we have become obsessed with their physical manifestation and adopted extreme assumptions about perfection and enlightenment, such as:

- We cannot reach enlightenment until we become perfectly generous, happy to give even our flesh to a hungry dog. If we cannot imagine this, we are not yet fit for enlightenment.
- We cannot reach enlightenment until we perfect our morality, following each and every rule that society imposes on us, even as they change day by day. If we don't follow all of the rules, we will never reach enlightenment.
- We cannot reach enlightenment until we are perfectly patient, happy to wait for nirvana until each and every person in the world realizes it first. If we lack this perfect patience then we are not fit for enlightenment.
- We cannot reach enlightenment until we have perfect virtuous effort and are satisfied to do any task, never tiring. If we tire or become dissatisfied, we are not fit to attain enlightenment.

- We cannot reach enlightenment until we have perfected our concentration. Our minds must never stray from the absolute. If we take too much notice of the world around us, we are not fit to attain enlightenment.
- We cannot reach enlightenment until we have perfect wisdom. We are not omniscient; therefore we are obviously not worthy of enlightenment.

When you think about it in these terms, enlightenment starts sounding a lot more like a prison camp than paradise. It is no wonder that no one is in a hurry to arrive there. Who could live up to these standards?

The historical Buddha left in the night unannounced, abandoning his wife and newborn son to seek liberation from suffering. How's that for morality? Generosity? Patience? The Buddha was as enlightened as one man can get and yet he was still a man. Don't ever let scholars or fanatics tell you otherwise. Buddha was human, just like you. Just like you he wanted to be free from the suffering of the world. You don't believe that you can have lasting happiness because you don't live up to the generally accepted model of perfection? Well, neither did he. The only difference is, he got over that belief.

We, too, must let go of simplistic expectations of bodily and behavioral perfection. The popular Buddhist interpretations of the perfections—generosity, morality, patience, effort, concentration, and wisdom—are all qualities that need to be worked at, they are all considered valuable, and they are all just ideas that we have created.

But if we look beyond the physical manifestations of these qualities, we discover that their true essence— impermanence, freedom, causality, perseverance, being, and unity—are in the basic qualities that we possess naturally. We present these "backdoor" perfections to you here. No one constructed them. There's nothing you need to do to acquire them. You don't have to work for them. If you simply acknowledge them and give them some thought, you'll recognize that there's another basic quality innate to us: enlightenment. Once we look beyond the physical manifestation of the six qualities, we find something amazing: a guide to our ultimate nature, a long-forgotten map leading step-by-step to the greatest treasure in the world, enlightened realization.

This is not a Buddhist book or even a religious book. It's a book about seeing the world without limitations. This is a practical guide to living your life's fullest potential right now, no matter what your religion, your location, or how much money you have. It is about things we all have a right to: peace, abundance, freedom, the fruit of our labors, and our free will. We all have the right to see ourselves as part of a global community and we have the right to simply exist. Claiming those freedoms can change your life forever.

The nomad in the desert was thirsty, so he drank. The Buddha wanted to wake up from his dream of suffering, and so he realized enlightenment. He struggled for years, but when he finally gave up the distractions and temptations to tame the physical world, he sat down and just did it.

THE BACKDOOR APPROACH: ENLIGHTENMENT NOW

Everyone dreams of a better life. All the things you've ever wanted—happiness, loving relationships, health, abundance, and peace of mind—are all qualities of enlightenment, a way of embracing our fullest potential that seemed unavailable to us, until now.

In "The Backdoor Approach" section of each chapter, you will utilize the ideas you have learned in practical ways to change your life. Use the backdoor approach to reach any goal you desire. Simply build your understanding, step-by-step, chapter by chapter. Even if you don't know what you want, taking the steps in the "Backdoor Approach" can serve as a general tune-up for your well-being, reducing your hardship and opening your life to happiness and prosperity.

To live an enlightened life, you don't have to follow rules, radically change your behavior, or adopt a new belief system. The world of enlightenment is there for you to see with your own eyes and interpret with your own mind. All you have to do is wake up. Need a little help?

As Otto and Hannah discover the lost panels, we will examine this ancient wisdom and explore ways to use it to change the world. But after that, living an enlightened life will be up to you.

THE ESSENCE OF ENLIGHTENMENT NOW

"Don't mind the walls and guards; walk right past them. They cannot keep you from the spring."

- **The Backdoor to Enlightenment** is a method to realize enlightenment by recognizing how six perfect qualities exist in your life and environment.
- **The Backdoor Approach**
  All the things you've ever wanted—happiness, loving relationships, health, abundance, and peace of mind—are all qualities of enlightenment, a way of embracing our fullest potential. The backdoor approach is a step-by-step process to use these truths to transform your life.
- **Benefits** The backdoor to enlightenment
  - offers immediate realization
  - is a secular method of self-improvement that does not rely on or conflict with faith, mysticism, or a belief in any religion
  - can be applied to achieve any goal you desire: happiness, health, love, abundance, fame, and enlightenment.
- **Conclusion** To live an enlightened life, you don't have to follow rules, radically change your behavior, or adopt a new belief system. The world of enlightenment is there for you to see with your own eyes and interpret with your own mind.

The world is full of suffering; it is also full of overcoming it.

—HELEN KELLER

"Ow!" Hannah dropped the teapot and worn oven mitt and brought her burnt finger to her lips. "Stupid," she mumbled into the phone she cradled between her shoulder and chin. She stretched the phone cord to the kitchen sink where she plunged her finger into a stream of cool water.

"What?" a voice on the other end of the phone line complained.

"Not you, Mom. I just burned myself." Hannah studied her finger through the water and saw a blister rising eerily from the flesh.

"Put butter on it," her mother instructed.

Hannah smiled. "Good idea," she said, knowing both that it wasn't a good idea, and that there was no point in arguing with her mother. Now that she finally had her own apartment—her own tiny 1950s kitchen with her own secondhand teapot where she could burn her very own fingers—she could afford to patronize her mother; she was finally free to do whatever she wanted to do. "So you were saying? About Dad?"

"The doctor said if your father would have taken care of his diabetes, he wouldn't be in this position."

"So? Everyone knows doctors make the worst patients."

"So they're talking about surgery."

"Who is? Not Dad. He'd never agree to be on the other side of the knife. I know that's not what he wants."

"He's bad, Hannah. He never gets out of bed anymore. Since he retired, it's like he's lost interest in life. These ministrokes he's having, the next one could kill him. He won't even eat anything now."

"Dad won't eat? I bet if you put a plate of blintzes and sour cream in front of him . . ." Hannah stretched the phone cord to its utmost to the bathroom medicine cabinet. Found a Band-Aid, no butter, and then flopped down on her sofa. Someday she'd have an apartment so big she'd need a cordless phone.

"We can't let him do that to himself anymore, and he said he'd rather starve than go on the diet the hospital recommended." Something in the way her mother said "starve" sounded small, serious, and it painfully put Hannah's newfound independence into perspective.

"I'm moving back home," Hannah decided.

"Don't be ridiculous. You've been dreaming about being the librarian at that place since you read Drake's books in high school. You've had the job for less than a month and now you want to come home? Your dad will be fine. We just need to get him in for a tune-up."

Hannah sighed. "Can I talk to him?"

"He's asleep, honey. I'll tell him you said hi."

Her father was growing old, he was sick, and despite her mother's optimism, it was only a matter of time before he was going to die. She always felt perfectly confident in the world, knowing she could rely on her father's love and support to make any size problem seem bearable. If she didn't have him, Hannah would feel alone and unprotected. As Hannah bandaged her finger, she couldn't help thinking about the backdoor to enlightenment panels. What if there was something written in them that could help him get better? Maybe even if he took an interest in them, it might bring him enough out of his apparent depression to save himself.

"Tell him about the package I found at the library," Hannah said. "He loves learning about this kind of stuff."

"Buried treasures?" her mother guessed, hitting on one of her father's passions, for sure: making money. Hannah laughed with tears in her eyes remembering how incorrigible he could be when he was healthier. Once when she asked him to take a trip to Italy with her, he told her he had no intentions of taking a day off work until he was 150. He joked that he had already spent the money. But Hannah was thinking of a different fascination that drove him to study medicine, one that might be in the forefront of his mind now that he was ill.

"No," Hannah said, "I'm talking about his other obsession, finding the meaning of life."

The Philosophical Study Center Library was not a lending library and yet, on this night, a whole stack of books had gone truant at the ambitious hands of Otto Mackenzie. Copies of *Steganographia* and *Polygraphia* by Trithemius, *The Secret and Swift Messenger* by John Wilkins, as well as many other rare and old volumes littered his kitchen table, sprung free until morning by the very librarian charged with keeping them safe inside the library.

Working steadily through a case of Guinness, Otto read about codes and cryptograms from the old masters of the art and tried his hand cracking the message before him with every method available. Numerical codes, literal and biliteral codes, acromatic, and musical. He ignored the most complex. He had to assume, if there was indeed a code, that Drake *wanted* it to be broken. According to these books, if Drake intended to hide his secret forever, there were countless ways to do the trick. All night Otto worked and drank, trying method after method, until finally he passed out at the table, his forehead pressed against the open pages of Ethan Allen Hitchcock's *Red Book of Appin*, with the lights from the philosophy library shining into his apartment from across the elm-lined street.

When the phone rang, startling Otto enough to nearly knock the dregs of a warm beer onto Athanasius Kircher's *Oedipus Aegypticus*, he prayed it was a telemarketer or a misdirected fax. Again and again it sounded, the LED lighting up blue with an urgency usually reserved for ambulance lights. Otto blurred his focus, lest he catch a glimpse of the caller ID and lose his nerve. He picked it up.

He cleared his throat and tried to sound sober. "Yes?"

"I know it must be late there, I'm sorry, but I had to call and give you the news," a woman's voice sounded from the other end.

"It's not mine?" Otto said wryly.

"Very funny, mister. No. I just left the imaging center. It's a little boy!"

"I guess we'll have to stop calling it *It*. Congratulations, Chloe."

"I can have my brother paint the room now. Not pink."

"Thank God for small miracles," he said.

"Maybe turquoise, like the sea." She paused. "Otto, I was thinking, there's no reason you couldn't come home. You're going to be thirty-three this year. Maybe it's time to settle down."

"Oh don't start, Chloe. This is my home." Otto surveyed his tidy studio apartment: microwave, sink, freshly painted cabinets, computer on a desk complete with wheels, futon-slash-sofa. Quilt hand-assembled by Mum. "I know we are no longer calling it—him—a mistake, but I'm still terribly sorry about what happened. I like you a great deal; I have since we were kids, but I'm not in love with you, whatever that means."

"Otto, I'm not saying—"

"Let me finish. I'm not ready to be a father. I know there are great responsibilities associated with that title, and I'm simply not up to snuff. I realize that I'm not doing the right thing. That I'm being an arse. But you know me. I came back to Devon for a holiday, not to become a bloody patriarch. This is what you wanted, Chloe, and you are on your own."

They were both silent for a moment and then Chloe spoke. "I just thought you'd want to know, that's all."

"Yes, well, thank you," Otto said, finding his civility. "Now if you'll excuse me, I'm in the middle of something."

"I'm sorry I bothered you. I didn't realize you were drinking," she said and hung up.

Otto lowered the phone onto its cradle. He leaned back in his chair, surveying his apartment again from the fresh perspective of a drunken man who had just burned the last ties to the only woman he had ever cared for, and was now likely never to know his own son: table full of bottles, empty refrigerator, empty cupboards. He reconsidered his futon-slash-bed. When was the last time he had fallen asleep anywhere but at his computer or at the table? Drowning in a never-ending stream of work and lager, he knew that no matter how hard he tried, he'd never be able to keep up with either.

Something about Chloe's words stung him. How did he get to be an adult? A third of his life was over, and he was in this apartment, miles away from anyone who loved him, working a job that meant nothing to him. Any thought of the future terrified him.

He reconsidered the books on the table. This little find had meant so much to him just a few hours before. He had imagined how different his life would be if he could learn old Drake's secret to enlightenment. What better way to prove to himself that he was smart, worthwhile, than to solve the greatest mystery in the world? He now laughed bitterly at his previous thoughts of fame and recognition, and collected the books.

One was a book by Drake himself. Otto opened to the frontispiece and looked at the portrait. "You got me, Drake, old man. I'm just the guy who pastes up newsletters and fixes typos on your Web site." He scanned the text beneath the photo. "Who was I to think I could find the backdoor to enlightenment, whatever that is? I'm nobody. It says here you were a thirty-third-degree Freemason." He closed the book. "Well, good for you. I'm a thirty-three-year-old drunk."

"Wait a second." There was that number again. Thirty-three. He opened the book before him to page 33. In the margin was a faint stamp. RLD. Robert Lewis Drake. He opened another to page 33. There it was again. And another.

"And you hid it in cabinet thirty-three? Pretty important number to you, eh? It couldn't be that simple," Otto said aloud. But as he circled every thirty-third word of Drake's translation, he realized that it was.

"Are you making this up?" Hannah whispered over her desk the next day at work. The library had few patrons that afternoon, but Hannah was buried in research. There simply weren't enough hours in the day to keep up with all the requests that crossed her desk. Her assistant, the elderly Mrs. Granger, only came in three days a week, and she didn't move fast enough to be much of a help. Hannah pushed all the books and notes aside and took the pages that Otto offered her.

"Check it yourself," Otto said.

Hannah put on her glasses and did just that. There it was, clear as day. A message from Robert Drake telling them where to find the secret backdoor to enlightenment:

"Many thirst for the great secret but can't taste the spring without proper reason. My friend, strive to avoid both lean-

ings and the word written within again must unlock the backdoor."

"Does this mean anything to you?" Otto asked.

"Apparently it's another test. If we don't have the right motivation to seek enlightenment—"

"Or even know what it is," Otto interrupted.

"Then we're done," Hannah finished. "Got any ideas?"

"The proper motivation to seek enlightenment. It's one word. *The word written within*, and it's in these pages."

"Piety?" Hannah tried. "Just being a good person, or wanting to, is that a good reason?"

"Apparently not good enough," Otto said, scanning the translation. "Piety's not in there. What about *curiosity?"*

"Oh that's a good one. 'I'm just curious, but what is the meaning of life?' " Hannah mocked.

"World domination? I suppose that's two words," Otto said.

A young patron in a baseball cap shot Otto a look. Hannah shook her head.

"Smarty-pants. Then you have a go," Otto said.

"Okay, well what about the opportunity to help everyone else achieve enlightenment? What would that be called?"

"One word?" Otto asked. Hannah nodded.

"Tedious," Otto decided. "And that's not in there either."

"Could you please keep it down," a skinny old man in tweed hissed at him.

"That's the guy with all the Freemason books. He's right, though. We can't do this now. Leave these with me. I'll see if I can work some old-fashioned librarian magic."

"Want to meet after work?" Otto asked.

"After Emma leaves." Hannah motioned to the ageless Asian woman seated behind the large desk in the next room. "If she catches wind of this, game over."

Emma, it turned out, didn't pose a problem that afternoon. She left shortly after yelling at Otto for delaying the bulletins. When five o'clock rolled around, Otto was so interested to see if Hannah was able to find anything, he didn't even pack up any work to take home with him.

"So?" he asked her when they were finally alone.

Hannah smirked. "I got it. Everything I read stated the fact very clearly. The Buddha had only one motivation to achieve enlightenment."

"Which is?"

"Which is that the world sucks. There's sickness, aging, death, mislaid values, constant change, and just plain stupidity everywhere you look. If that isn't reason enough to look for a better way, I don't know what is."

"You'll have no argument from me, though I think 'world domination' has a better ring to it. But what's the word we're looking for? I can't see old Drake typing in 'sucks.'"

"Suffering," Hannah said, handing him the translation. "It's in there."

"Oh, that would explain the golden wheel. It's the wheel of the cycle of suffering."

"You could have mentioned that earlier. But before you get too excited, I still have no idea where he put the rest of the panels. '*Strive to avoid both leanings and the word written within again must unlock the backdoor.*' Does that mean anything to you?"

"Yeah actually it does. From what I remember in my A levels, the path to enlightenment is the middle way, the path between hard-core asceticism and indulgence. So don't go to extremes. That's all."

"Otto, that doesn't help us."

" '*The word written within.*' Maybe it's time for us to take another look at the original."

Up in the Art Annex they examined the original translation of the panel on the light table, examining the word *suffering* with a magnifying glass.

"Oh no," Otto said when he saw the word, his heart sinking. "If you look closely there are three kinds of fonts here in this one word."

"How can you tell?" Hannah said, squinting.

"Because see this first *f* is different from the second and some of the letters seem italicized ever so slightly."

Hannah took a closer look.

"Oh yeah," she said.

"I was reading about this last night. It's called a biliteral, or in this case, triliteral cipher. Three different alphabets are used. Each letter of each alphabet used breaks down into a value of *a* or *b*. It takes a combination of five *a*s and *b*s to make one letter, and then the final message is revealed using a disc cipher."

"Are you done?" Hannah asked.

"Yes. Quite. I'm ready to hand over the panel to Emma the dragon lady and get back to my life of suffering, thanks."

"Good, because I just solved the code."

"Really?"

"Drake said to *strive to avoid both leanings*. It's not a triliteral code. The italics bend to the right, these other letters curve to the left. If you eliminate those *leaning* letters, you're left with—" she said.

"*SEIG*. These are the letters that are left."

"Look again. The *i* is actually a small number one and the *g*—"

"It's an eight. I see it now, *SE18*. That's better somehow?"

"It's a call number in the wacky world of Drake's library. The Dewey decimal system was beneath him, apparently."

Among the books of secret societies and secular humanism, *SE18* stood out as an impossibly tall, thin rebound volume of *Cryptomenytices et Cryptographiae*, by Gustavus Selenus.

"Not another puzzle," Hannah sighed.

"No. Look at the shape of the book. The panel is in the binding," Otto said. "It has to be. Take it apart."

"Take it apart? What if it's not in there?" Hannah said.

"Then you'll be a bad, bad librarian, and my hands will still be clean."

Something about his tone made what she was about to do less horrific and more fun.

"I need something to cut the endleaf from the cover . . ." Before Hannah could finish, Otto flipped open a pocketknife and placed it in her hand.

"Back from the old days when I had a real job," Otto explained.

"Front or back?" Hannah painfully deliberated where she would make her first incision on the book.

"Backdoor, ain't it? Back cover," Otto declared.

Hannah put the knife to the paper and then hesitated. "For the record," she said, "I would never do this to the original binding."

"Just cut it!" Otto cried out.

She did and there it was, thinner than she imagined, another panel wrapped in the familiar brown paper.

In that moment, in their excitement, the suffering of the world receded and was replaced by a flood of hope and wonder.

ILLUMINATING SUFFERING

If you stop all your actions for a moment and examine your state of being, how do you really feel? Do you feel like you are fighting an uphill battle? Like no matter how much you do, there will always be something left undone? Do you feel that the forces in the world are slowly wearing you down?

Do you know why you have those sneaking suspicions and uncomfortable notions? Because as unpopular and unpleasant as those ideas are, they are all true. You heard right: Life is a struggle.

There is a strange trend in society to act as if these truths don't exist. The suffering in the world is a problem that appears so insurmountable, sometimes we think our only option is to ignore it and hope it will go away. Certainly you can stay busy acquiring things and doing activities to take your mind off the situation, but at the end of the day, you will be tired. At the beginning of the next day, you will wake up tired. And at the end of all your tired days, you will be shocked to learn that your life is over. That's the way you've lived until now, but there is another way.

By realizing how we already live in an enlightened state, we can transcend the struggles that permeate our lives, and embrace more prosperity, peace, and happiness than we could ever imagine. We can live the lives we've always dreamed.

Enlightenment is not an action; it is an understanding that allows us *to transcend the suffering of the world*. The backdoor is an instantaneous route to that state, but before we see beyond the obstacles to achieve our dreams, we must take an honest inventory of the human condition and identify precisely what is holding us back. Then our enlightened lives—our true lives—can begin to unfold.

The first type of suffering we have to deal with is physical pain. Here we are talking about the common sensation Hannah experienced when she burned herself on the teapot. The primary source of suffering, pain, is something even the most basic organisms with a nervous system will try to avoid. We cannot avoid the pain impulse; it is, however, often exacerbated by stress and drama. But pain is a bigger part of our everyday lives than we care to admit.

Pain is uncomfortable, but it's not such a bad thing. In fact, if it weren't uncomfortable, it wouldn't work as well as it does. The pain impulse alarms you when you are hungry, when you are injuring yourself, and when your temperature reaches a dangerous level. It is the way your nervous system communicates your body's needs to your brain. It teaches you which activities are safe for your body and which are harmful.

When the nervous system is incapacitated, terrible things happen. An example of this is the bacterial infection leprosy. The bacillus attacks the nerve endings and destroys the body's ability to feel pain. Without feeling pain, people with leprosy easily injure themselves by doing things they take for granted every day: scratching an itch, holding a cup of hot coffee, wearing uncomfortable shoes, and chewing food. These injuries become infected, and without pain to remind people that they are injured, their condition worsens. Ultimately, disfigurement results. Pain is the way your body communicates its limits to your mind throughout the day. The experience of pain is a natural part of life.

The second type of suffering, *discontent*, is dissatisfaction, a craving for something one does not have. It is the failure to realize when enough is enough, and it is one of the most important challenges facing the world today.

Hannah's ailing father suffers from some of the most familiar forms of discontent: greed and pride. A lifetime of overindulgence has destoyed his health, and yet he continues to do the things that made him ill. Greed is a demonstration of obsessive behavior and unhealthy attachment. When you succumb to greed the things that are supposed to make you happy have the potential to make you the most miserable. Even with expert advice and his own training as a medical doctor, his discontent was stronger than his will to resist it. Maybe he picked up terrible eating habits as he worked nights, obsessed with making more and more money. He said it was for his family's sake, but Hannah and her brother always had everything they wanted, and if you asked them, they would say they would have been happier to spend more time with their father.

Once he found himself living overweight with uncontrolled diabetes, he might have recovered had he not also suffered from a terrible case of pride: an attachment to status, an addiction to importance, or even an obsession with self. He was unable to see himself and his position in the world accurately. He craved admiration for his expertise, and he couldn't admit that someone might know better about his health than he did. He consistently refused treatment and his health declined. Discontent could very well cost Hannah's father his life.

On individual levels, discontent creates stress in our lives. This affects our sleep, our happiness, and, like Hannah's dad, our health. Socially, discontent is ruining our relationships with our spouses, our children, our families and friends. We've all been in a place when our expectations of others have exceeded their abilities, and we've all been in a situation when a loved one has demanded more than a reasonable share of our time or resources. Historically, wanting more than our fair share has led clans, tribes, and nations to war. Environmentally, politically, and culturally, if everyone were satisfied with what they needed, rather than what they wanted, we would be living in a much happier world.

We consume more than we need and more than is healthy. Obesity is quickly becoming an epidemic in some countries, while much of the world's population is underfed or starving. A fraction of the world's population is consuming a lion's share of the world's goods. When something breaks, it's often cheaper and less of a hassle to replace it than fix it. Just buy a new one. Our clothes go out of fashion *every season*. Just buy new ones. Our furnishings go out of style. Our houses get old. We just buy new ones.

We act as if the primary purpose of a human being is to process goods into garbage. The more expensive and plentiful the goods that we are able to convert into trash per year, the more successful we feel. We feel pressured to consume more and more every day, and work harder to keep up with our consumption. Meanwhile our lives are passing by.

The third type of suffering is the *suffering of constructs*. Our minds create elaborate ideas and objects (constructs) that tend to cause us a tremendous amount of discomfort. Everything in our society has been assembled from what was here before. Houses, bridges, roads—things you are used to thinking of as constructs—but so are sports, language, music, and romantic love. The list is endless: Nature is not a human construct, but our ideas about it are. Outer space might not be a human construct, but the only way you are capable of thinking about it is. We build ideas. We build rules. We build cultures. We build governments. We'd like to believe our constructs are permanent, fundamental, and universal, but they are all simply something someone thought up.

Thinking and creating are the most treasured things in life. We are going to have some great ideas, we are going to have some dumb ones, and we are going to have a whole lot of average ones in between. We are going to create some masterpieces and tools that will make our lives easier, and we are all going to create tons and tons of garbage. In the long run, we create and think up plenty of everything. The constructs aren't the problem. This type of suffering consists of all the ways we use our own ideas and decisions to make ourselves feel trapped and awful.

Otto has a real problem with his constructs. He cares for Chloe, but not only have his ideas about love and responsibility kept him from making a commitment to her; they have driven him out of his country, far enough away to feel safe from the expectations he is certain she must have of him. When a brief reunion resulted in Chloe's pregnancy, his ideas about what a parent should be make him feel even more trapped and overwhelmed. He has a very clear idea about what is moral, and he's angry that he can't live up to his own standard. When Chloe reaches out to him, he is argumentative and defensive, not because of what she says or does but because of what he believes she must feel—based on his own expectations. He feels conflicted; he has been presented a rare opportunity for happiness, but his beliefs about love, morality, and parenthood have paralyzed him and made him bitter. If he can't live up to his own standards, he will punish himself. His life, he has decided, will be nothing but drudgery and labor.

His only solace, he has decided, will be to pickle his problems in alcohol. This is what he believes men do—though if he had grown up in different circumstances, he could have easily turned to drugs, sex, or some other addiction.

Does Otto's fear of responsibility warrant an empty life of low-paying jobs and liver disease? Who knows, but that's the thing about mental constructs, they are arbitrary. There's no court out there to determine if his ideas about himself are fair.

The fourth type of suffering is *pervasive action*. Action is present throughout all existence. Forces work upon and influence one another in a great mix of activity and change. Being trapped in this system can make us feel impotent, out of control, and angry. Being born into this world of never-ending change is like finding ourselves suddenly hurtling through a busy street on a speeding motorcycle with unfamiliar controls. As obstacles and threats zoom by or slam into us, we struggle to steer, slow down, or just get off the bike. The suffering of pervasive action is the anxiety of that struggle.

Getting hit in the face with the debris as you watch life rocket by is enough to make anyone feel frustrated or hopeless, or look for creative answers in the wrong places. Hannah has noticed this discomfort in her life. At her job, for every question she answers with hours of research, there are always three more being submitted. How is she ever supposed to keep up? She hasn't even gotten to the point in her life where she might worry about getting behind in her bills, housework, when appliances will break one after another and her new car will need repair. Someday she will have children who will get the flu, need a ride to ballet lessons, and expect to eat dinner every night. How is Hannah supposed to get a sense of control or power when she feels helpless and insignificant in the face of all that chaos?

Finally, the most persistent type of suffering we endure is *ignorance*, a simple lack of understanding. From the beginning, ignorance has haunted man. Man's caution concerning the unknown has served him well and kept him from harm, but it is always what we don't know that hurts us. Through logical and scientific reasoning, we are able to chip away at the great body of unknowns that stands between us and safety, but on some level, we will always have ignorance. As we learn the rules, the rules change. We cure old diseases, and new ones are born. Our solutions to old problems create new ones.

Hannah and Otto are struggling with ignorance in different ways, both resulting in fear. Hannah is afraid for her father's life for many reasons. She loves him, so she wants him to enjoy a long and full life. If he dies she will miss him terribly, and she is terrified to be responsible for her own welfare. She feels she's off to a good start—she's out of college and happy, if not a little overwhelmed at her first real job—but what if something goes wrong? What if she's faced with a problem she can't handle? She can't imagine living her life without the safety net that her father has always provided.

Hannah is also afraid of failure. This fear has made her downscale her goals and kept her from going after the career she really wants. Trivial ups and downs don't bother her, but when it comes to putting her dreams on the line, she'd rather never act on them—keeping them always as a possibility in her mind—than pursue them openly and risk failure.

Otto has his own set of fears. He knows he can take care of himself, but he is afraid he won't be able to provide for both Chloe and the child they are expecting. What if they need something that he can't provide? What if his relationship with Chloe turns as bitter as his own parents' relationship? His fears have made him lazy, depressed, and discouraged.

Chances are, at some time or another you have experienced each of these kinds of discomforts. You can deny it or choose to ignore it, but the unpleasant truth is, the world is full of suffering, death, and decline. But it is also a world full of life, growth, and enjoyment.

THE BACKDOOR APPROACH: UNLOCKING THE BACKDOOR

Once you admit that hardship exists in your life, you can go about the business of discovering how your own misunderstandings about the world create and contribute to many of them. This is the first step to the backdoor.

> Step One: IDENTIFY the different struggles
> that exist in your life.

Be open to the possibility that your struggles can be eliminated. Cultivate a desire to eliminate them. What a relief this is, instead of cowering and ignoring your struggles, you can face them, looking forward to the day when they will be no more. Write down all of the challenges you have in your life. Be thorough. Don't leave anything out. Now take that piece of paper and burn it. As you watch the smoke drift away, say good-bye to your old way of life and vow that you will not give up until your suffering dissipates like the smoke in the breeze. Now that you have formed a strong intention with an open mind, you can learn to transform the hours you spend struggling into hours of enjoyment. You can minimize the suffering you experience in the world until, liberated, you reach the backdoor to enlightenment.

THE ESSENCE OF UNLOCKING THE BACKDOOR

*"Many thirst for the great secret but can't taste
the spring without proper reason."*

- **Life is a struggle.** The different kinds of suffering
  include
  - **Pain:** physical discomfort
  - **Discontent:** dissatisfaction
  - **Constructs:** our own limiting ideas and attitudes
  - **Pervasive Action:** being trapped by the constant
    change of the world around us, and
  - **Ignorance:** lack of wisdom.
- **The Backdoor Approach**
  Step One: IDENTIFY the struggles in your life.
- **Exercise**   Write down all of the challenges you have
  in your life. Now take that piece of paper and burn
  it. Vow that you won't give up until your suffering
  dissipates like the smoke in the breeze.
- **Conclusion**   Once you acknowledge that suffering
  exists, you can begin to find ways to reduce it.

Oh, this is the joy of the rose:
That it blows,
And goes.

—WILLA CATHER

The perfection of impermanence | 2

"What on earth are you doing to that book?"

Mrs. Granger's flinty voice rang out across the darkened library, shocking Hannah enough that she quickly hid the knife in her pocket and closed the thin volume that contained the prize they sought. Otto's eyes darted to the shelves around them. There was no time to hide the evidence. They had been caught red-handed defacing library property.

Mrs. Granger was just as old and fragile as many of the books in the library, and she had been there longer than most.

"Someone left a piece of . . ." Hannah froze, unable to find the words to continue her lie.

"Tape," Otto said without skipping a beat. "A sticky nasty piece of tape on the book. I lent her my knife and now it's all sorted."

"All vandalized property must be submitted for restoration." Mrs. Granger stuck out her hand, nearly transparent with age. "Give it to me," she said. "I'll see that Emma gets it."

"It was a very small piece of tape. More of a piece of paper really." Otto backpedaled, taking the book from Hannah's trembling hands.

"These are very delicate books, Hannah. And they must be cared for properly," Mrs. Granger said. "You have no idea what you're dealing with."

"You're right, but I'm beginning to get a better idea of how important these books are," Hannah said, meaning it.

Mrs. Granger considered them both for a moment and took a golden key from her pocket and handed it to Hannah. "I'm glad you're finally taking an interest in our treasures. Now, why don't you do me a favor and leave that book in the repair bin when you're finished with it. It will save my knees a trip up those stairs."

Hannah looked at the gold key. The small silver-rimmed tag simply read *Access*.

"Access to what?" Hannah asked.

"To the upstairs office, my old office. I suppose it's your office now that you're librarian. It must have slipped my mind to give you the key."

"Sure it slipped her mind," Hannah said when she was out in the courtyard with Otto. The lemon trees were full of ripe fruit and the flowers were blooming. She could hardly contain her irritation. "That lady creeps me out. I need someone to help with the research, not look over my shoulder all the time. She's supposed to be my assistant. How's she assisting me?"

"Are you kidding? That dinosaur's been the librarian

since Drake opened the place back at the dawn of time. Drake's trust left some provision that the Wycombes had to keep her around as long as the library could afford to keep her. There's no way they can get her out without violating the trust. She watches the place like a hawk."

"So we're all stuck with her," Hannah summed up. "But it makes me feel a little better to know that she's a royal inconvenience to the Wycombes. So where do you want to read the rest of this?" Hannah thought to offer her apartment, which was less than a block away, but then thought Otto might think she was being forward.

"Don't know. There's a pub down the hill a bit. We could go there," Otto offered. After the run-in with Granger, he could use a drink.

"Like a bar? With drunk people? Are you crazy? Do you have any idea how valuable this is?"

"No need to get snarky. It was just a suggestion." Otto was secretly relieved and utterly satisfied to end up at Starbucks with Hannah and the secret to enlightenment. After they had nestled themselves in a corner with a strong cup of coffee in a couple of big velour armchairs, Hannah slipped the package out of her bag and presented it to Otto.

He weighed it in his hands.

"Feels a bit light, don't you think?" he said, a little disappointed.

"Maybe the secret to enlightenment is short. Concise." Hannah took the package back from him and picked at the twine with her short, sensibly trimmed fingernails. Once she managed to tease the knot loose, she joined Otto in his disappointment. "There's only one panel in here."

He leaned over to study the black panel in Hannah's lap. At the top a golden conch shell was delicately painted and then below, lines of text. Hannah carefully placed the panel aside to expose the translation handprinted on the outer wrapping paper.

> *A seeker who relies on objects and ideas to practice generosity is like someone walking in the dark; he will not see anything.*
>
> *Objects and ideas cloud his vision. If he does not depend on material things and ideas to practice generosity, he is like a man walking in the sun; he can see all shapes and colors. Richness, beauty, and complexity are only possible because of change. The potential for everything exists everywhere in an ever-shifting, impermanent world. To realize enlightenment, one must recognize that the true generous nature of all phenomena is the abundance of impermanence.*

And then below, Drake's instructions:

> *Don't let greed interfere with your progress. How can you ever be satisfied with many if you can't appreciate one? When you burn away your attachment to the things you*

hold, your path will be revealed. Be generous enough to al-
low impermanent things to be impermanent, and then you
will uncover the next verse.

"You've got to be kidding me," Otto huffed. "The *next*
verse? That means they're all hidden separately?"

"You said there were Six Perfections. Maybe there are
six panels," Hannah guessed.

Otto sat back in his chair, his head spinning. The possibilities were endless. After the fight he had had with
Emma over the bulletins and the conversation he had had
with Chloe, the only thing keeping him there was this
dream of discovering the rest of the hidden panels. But
Drake wasn't going to let him cash in so quickly. Otto saw
himself walking out of that coffee shop, gathering up his
few possessions, and moving east.

Then Hannah put her hand on his arm. She wanted to
comfort him, he knew, and if he covered her hand with
his, her innocent gesture could be the beginning of a
relationship. He then considered the panels. He might
never find another one, but to have that opportunity he
would have to stay, and it would be a lot easier—but less
fun—if they remained just friendly coworkers. He didn't
reach for her hand.

He watched his temper pass; he would not quit his job.
He saw only one option ahead of him now, and that was to
stay where he was and finish what he had started.

"I'm going to see my parents this weekend," Hannah said.

"Okay," Otto said, finishing his coffee. "I'll take a look at this and call you Sunday night. We'll find the rest of this thing."

The next morning Hannah took the four-hour drive up the coast. Her brother was helping her mom hang some shelves in the new guest room—which used to be Hannah's room. They had already bought a new bed and the pale blue walls that she had grown up with had been covered with grass cloth.

"There's no going back now," Andrew said and bent over to give his sister a consolatory squeeze. "Mom has decorated you out of her life."

"Actually, moving out for a few months was all part of my plan to update my room," Hannah joked. "Nice choices, Mom."

"Please, Hannah. Your father and I would like a few years alone before we die," Hannah's mom repeated the old family joke and then caught herself. Suddenly she looked as though she was going to cry. "I'm sorry," she whispered.

Hannah kissed her mom on the cheek.

"He's out back if you want to say hello," her mom said quietly.

Hannah found her father sitting out by the pool with an old plaid blanket draped over his shoulders, even though it was nearly eighty degrees.

"Hey, Kitten," he said. "You have a safe drive?"

"Yup," she said. He looked worse than she had imagined. His skin was grayish and he sat so still, Hannah wondered if he could move. "I can't believe you're letting Andrew hang shelves," Hannah said. "You know you're just going to have to fix them later."

"Those days are over, Hannah. I'm sure they'll be just fine." He quieted again. After a few minutes Hannah had to wonder if he had forgotten she was there, but then he looked at her as if he was seeing her for the first time. "You look so pretty." He shook his head. "I never thought I'd be this old."

"You're not that old," Hannah said, trying to hide a fat tear that hung in the corner of her eye.

"I'm old enough," he said decidedly. "Your mom told me you made an interesting discovery at that library."

Hannah was relieved to change the topic to more concrete things, words and ideas that she could use to bury her emotion. "Yeah, we found some ancient Tibetan text. *The Backdoor to Enlightenment*. Otto and I found the first two parts, but the rest is hidden somewhere in the library."

"Otto?" her father said with a smile.

"Just a guy who works there with me." No, she thought, with his rumpled oxford shirts and his nearly ten extra years, he'd be too easy. Plus he needed a haircut.

Hannah told her dad the story written in the first panels and all about their recent find. "So what do you think? Do you think it's really the secret to enlightenment?"

"Well, the first part sounds right to me," he said. "Life is full of suffering. I learned that lesson early, working in the ER. You wouldn't believe the tragedy I saw there. The worst of it from motorcycles. Never ride motorcycles, Hannah."

"Okay, Dad."

"So that part is right. But what about the other panel you found? You didn't explain that one," he said.

"I don't think I get it. That's why." She handed him a piece of paper. "I copied the message for you. The first one's there, too."

He took his glasses from his pocket and rested them on his nose. The arm was broken. He didn't seem to care. He read quietly for a moment.

"I wish I had read this forty years ago," Hannah's father said. "But I don't know if I would have understood it."

"You get it?"

"I understand it all too well. I spent my life learning it the hard way. This part," he pointed to the first few sentences:

A seeker who relies on objects and ideas to practice generosity is like someone walking in the dark; he will not see anything. Objects and ideas cloud his vision. If he does not depend on material things and ideas to practice generosity, he is like a man walking in the sun. He can see all shapes and colors.

"I spent my whole life thinking that by giving you kids whatever you wanted, making sure you had the best education, that I was being generous."

"You are, Dad. You're one of the most generous people I know."

"No. I was selfish and stupid. If I was really generous, I would have shared my attention with you, much more of my time, and my love."

"You love us, Dad."

"Of course I do, but for so many years I was so focused on other things that I didn't enjoy that love. I didn't take the time to enjoy you kids, and that's the truth."

Hannah had loved him her whole life. She always thought about him and did things to make him proud. Her love for him had given her years of joy. She didn't know what to say to this revelation that she hadn't been as big a part of her father's life as she had imagined, so she focused on the words in front of her.

"But what about this part? *'To realize enlightenment one must recognize that the true generous nature of all phenomena is the abundance of impermanence.'* " What is that supposed to mean?"

"That's the saddest part to realize this late in my life. You know what I was doing when you came out here?"

"Sleeping?" Hannah guessed.

"I was just watching the world rush by."

Hannah frowned. Maybe her mom was right, maybe her dad was losing it. "There's nothing going on out here, Dad."

"Isn't there? Look at the wind in the trees. Listen to it. The birds. The water glittering on the koi pond. Those scary fish poking their big orange heads out at me looking for a handout. The clouds. Smell the grass that your damn brother cut with that loud mower this morning while I was trying to sleep. And now you, sitting out here beside me. Don't say there's nothing going on. Every second there's a whole new world back here, and if you pay attention, there are hours in every second. That's pretty good news for a man in my position."

"How can you talk like that?"

"Because it's true. This old man's not going to be around much longer, Kitten. Those clouds aren't going to stand still. I'm going to die, and I wouldn't have it any other way. It's only because my life is coming to an end that I've been able to see how beautiful it all is. Here are the real riches. And I didn't have to waste years of my life working in an operating room to earn it. But I'll tell you what, even if you don't find any more of that book, what you found could be the most important discovery a person could make, at any age. If I had lived my whole life knowing what I know now, I wouldn't have missed a second with you kids. Watching you learn and grow, knowing each moment was so precious because it would never happen again. I can't even imagine if I had been able to live my whole life like that instead of just these last days."

"But what about the bad times? When you almost lost your practice? When mom was sick?"

"Some of the best times in my life were times that I thought were the worst. Your mother and I were never so close as in those months when we thought we were going to lose her. And I found strength I didn't know I had. The good, the bad—it's all precious because it all just passes by. Let go of your beliefs that any situation is permanent."

Hannah fought her emotion and sat for a moment to take in what her father was saying. The backyard was alive with hummingbirds and insects, and a million kinds of light all interplaying and shifting. They sat quietly together watching the clouds and feeling the wind and sun and cherishing the impermanence of it all until they were called in for dinner.

B ack in the city, Otto didn't have much time to investigate Drake's next clue. He had to spend the weekend getting caught up with his work.

An ever-shifting, impermanent world is right, Otto thought. When he had arrived in America, he had been impressed by Emma Wycombe's job offer. It didn't pay much, but he'd have the opportunity to be creative, designing all the materials for the lecture bulletins, gift shop catalogues, and Web site. Then Emma decided she would keep the format of the catalog the same and just change the cover each month. Next she stopped allowing him to alter the Web site unless it was to make corrections and updates. Finally, this week, she gave him a template for the bulletins. They would be the same every month; only the names and dates would change. He had never minded his job until he noticed how over the course of a few years his job had changed without his even realizing it.

Finding these panels was the most enjoyable thing to come his way at work in months. But this new clue, coupled with the unpleasant discovery that he'd have to keep looking for more panels, was really trying his patience. Studying the translation from the latest panel, he counted words and tried all the tricks he'd learned looking for the first clue, but to no avail. The only thing that seemed out of order with the clue was that, to his finely tuned nose, the old paper faintly smelled of lemons.

He cracked open a beer and left a message on Hannah's voice mail and waited for her to call him back. Even though he hadn't made any progress, he was still looking forward to hearing her voice.

He had always craved his independence above all things, that, and satisfying a desire to be unconventional. But where had it gotten him? None of his friends back home, not to mention Chloe, could believe it when he told them he was leaving his job and staying in America to work at a philosophy library. It was the last thing anyone would have expected from him. But now that he had his freedom, being alone wasn't as interesting to him as it once was. Drake's panels were right. Maybe things— even people and what they want—do change, he thought as he finished updating the Web site.

By the time Hannah returned his call, it was after ten. Even though he had only the most vague olfactory information to pass on to her, he offered to meet her at the library that night. It would be sc-sc-scary there at night, he promised, and so she agreed.

"Lemons?" she said. "This doesn't smell like anything but old paper."

The library definitely had a different personality late at night. The moonlight coming in the skylight gave everything a peculiar glow, and the big wooden table looked like an altar for pagan rituals. Otto was right. It was spooky.

"No. This is definitely citrus. Maybe lime?" he asked himself and took another sniff. "No, lemons."

"Are you like part dog or something?"

"Everyone's got their gifts," he said. "Just because I don't have your long eyelashes and pretty smile . . ."

"I don't have long eyelashes," Hannah said, a little glad he had noticed.

"You do, lassie. And I'll do you one better, you know

you do 'cause you're always batting them around when you want something. Now all I've got is this superior nose, and when it tells me lemons, I tend to believe it."

"Well then," Hannah said. "I would have said your best quality was your pretty blue eyes, but if you have faith in your nose . . ."

"Which says lemons," Otto reminded her.

"Then we have to ask ourselves if that trick we did as kids using lemon juice like invisible ink still works," Hannah said, impressed with her recall. "Maybe that was how Drake hid this clue."

"You wrote in lemon juice? Really? Like secret messages?"

"Of great importance, such as sending notes to my best friend asking if her brother liked me."

"No doubt he did. You probably batted those eyelashes of yours at him until he forgot that you could be so cheeky. But how did your friend uncover your message?"

"I don't remember. I think you can develop the hidden message with vinegar maybe? Or salt? Are you sure you smell lemons? Whatever we do to this page will destroy it."

"Don't let greed interfere with your progress," Otto scolded her.

"It says 'burn away.' Want to try burning it? Maybe that would work."

"Why don't you Google that while I go to the Art Annex and make us a delicious cup of instant coffee?"

"Coffee? It's late."

"We're young," Otto said and went to plug in the electric kettle.

Hannah worked at her desk for a few minutes searching the Internet for invisible ink recipes. After she found what she was looking for, she joined Otto on a bench in front of a large replica of Raphael's *School of Athens*. In the center Plato stood with his finger pointing up to the heavens.

"I love this painting," Hannah said, taking the cup Otto offered her. "It's the only replica Drake has in the whole place. 'Here's where the truth lies,' Plato is telling Aristotle standing beside him, 'in the spiritual realm, in the unseen.' "

"And not to be bullied, Aristotle points to the ground. 'Not a chance, old man,' Aristotle is saying," Otto retorted. " 'The truth is right here on earth, in the things we see and do every day.' They've been at an impasse now in that painting for six hundred years."

"I didn't know you studied art," Hannah said, a little impressed.

"Field trip to the Vatican in high school. Did you know they let sixteen-year-olds drink in Italy?" Otto informed her.

"Fascinating," Hannah said with some sarcasm. "If

you're still interested, we can develop a message written in lemon juice with an iodine solution or, as Drake suggests, a flame."

"How does that work?"

"Trust me?" Hannah asked.

"Why not."

Hannah took a match from her pocket, lit it, and held the flame a few inches behind the page. She waved it back and forth until a small section of the page turned brown and began to smolder.

"Careful there," Otto said.

"It's okay. The lemon juice weakens the paper and will burn first." Light brown letters developed on the page: AA45.

"Another book?" Otto said.

"No, it's here in this room. Art Annex. AA. Forty-five is the flat file number, but there's no item number."

"Where's drawer forty-five?" Otto asked.

"I don't know," Hannah said, moving about the perimeter of the room reading the numbers on the big flat-file drawers. The numbers stop at forty-four."

Otto opened the last drawer and checked under a stack of watercolors. "It's not here."

"I just told you that," Hannah said in a daze, a horrible thought dawning on her. She turned slowly around to face the center of the room and the fantastic piece of art that stood there.

One of the library's most popular items, a six-foot-diameter circular Tibetan sand mandala, stood on a platform under a Plexiglas box. Many different colors of finely crushed stone had been meticulously laid down using tubes, funnels, and scrapers to form an elaborate pattern of squares within squares, a picture of a conch shell at the center.

"Oh no," Otto said, following her gaze. He checked the small plaque on the floor. " *'AA45. The Mandala of Abundance.'* There is no way Drake hid it in there."

"The Tibetan symbol of impermanence," Hannah said. " *'Allow impermanent things to be impermanent, and then you will uncover the next verse.'* A sand mandala is a perfect example of this. Once it has been built and viewed by the public, to complete the ceremony it's supposed to be destroyed."

"I feel sick," Otto said. He walked around the platform crouching every few feet to try to peek below it.

"What are you doing?" Hannah asked him.

"Maybe there's a door or a little slide-away panel," Otto said hopefully.

Hannah laughed. "It's under the sand, Otto. I got the last one. This one is all you."

"There is no way we can do this. This is criminal. It's like violating the terms of my visa," And then in the same breath, "Help me move this giant plastic box."

They moved the box aside and stood surveying the artwork. It was even more glorious and vibrant out in the open.

"This sand is two inches thick in some places. The panel could be under any of it," Otto said.

"Then you better get started. Come on, Otto, be generous."

"Cheeky." Otto cupped his hand at one corner of the largest square within the circle. "I need a drink," he said, took a deep breath, and swept his hand through the sand to the center.

"Oh my God, I can't believe you did that," Hannah blurted out.

"Are you serious?" Otto asked.

Hannah smiled. "No. Did you feel anything?"

"No. I think we're about to be fired for no reason."

"This time, *my* hands are clean," Hannah said, a little giddy.

Otto repeated the sweep from each corner. Nothing. He dug around in the pile in the center. Somewhere at the bottom his hands touched paper. A package. He lifted it out from the colored sand, held it up for Hannah to see, and let himself fall facedown on the ruined treasure, unable to believe what he had just done.

"That actually felt really good," he said.

ILLUMINATING IMPERMANENCE

Impermanence. Does that word sound ominous? Like it's a threat? An enemy we need protection from? After all, impermanence is responsible for aging and death, for prohibiting us to hold on forever to the things we love. Maybe instead of talking about how perfect impermanence is, we should all be filling up sandbags, to keep out the impermanence that threatens to seep in and destroy the stability we try so hard to establish.

Or maybe not. Impermanence is the name of the game in this world we live in. There is great benefit in realizing the extent to which change exists in the world: Acknowledging impermanence is critical if you want to eliminate suffering and realize enlightenment. Living with this simple realization will bring a natural openness, a willingness to give and receive without obligation or expectation, which eliminates the needless suffering of attempting to make permanent attachments to impermanent things.

The potential for everything exists everywhere, and within that potential is a range of probabilities. Our observations and our own reactions are what lock those probabilities into a single value or reality. We have the potential to do many things with the next hour of our lives. As each second goes by, the actions we take limit those probabilities until we have exhausted the hour and locked into an actuality. At each instant, our observation and reaction could nail down a completely new future.

Prompted by his disappointment, Otto became aware of this phenomenon when he and Hannah unwrapped their latest find at Starbucks. He was overwhelmed with the possibilities for his future. His situation and character made a number of those possibilities more probable than others. He was angry, so his first thought went to quitting his job, moving away. If he couldn't find what he was looking for, what was the use of staying? If he had chosen this path, he could have followed it anywhere in the world. But he ruled out that prospect when Hannah touched his arm. His reaction also prompted him to explore the new possibility of beginning a relationship with her. Finally, catching a glimpse of the panel, he remembered his original goal. Despite his slow progress, Otto made a decision that would shape his future: He would continue to search for the remaining panels.

The world is filled with more possibilities and potential than we could ever perceive or explore, and yet if we don't open our minds to the perfection of impermanence, we can limit ourselves to feeling trapped and bored. We only experience beauty, complexity, and richness because nothing is permanent. When you deny or refuse to accept the full impact of how change influences your world, you limit the richness you perceive.

Hannah's father spent many years of his life ignoring the impermanence of his life, his children's lives, and the world around him. Life seemed simple, if not a little dull. He thought he had it all figured out. All he had to do, he imagined, was earn enough money to give his family everything he thought they deserved and try to ease his discontent. He always imagined he had plenty of time, that the kids would always be children, and his life would be there waiting for him as soon as he quenched his urges for material things. When his failing health forced him to examine his life, he realized that in ignoring the countless small changes that happen every day, he had overlooked the richness and complexity that could have satisfied his discontent.

Enlightened minds recognize that nothing in the world we see around us is permanent, and this understanding helps them to avoid the common human discomfort of obsession and discontent. How? Discontent is a symptom of recognizing impermanence in what we have, but failing to recognize it in what we want. When we see something we want—a computer, a new jacket, a potential mate—it appears shiny and new, and we imagine that it will stay that way forever. But as soon as we possess it, we see how it changes both physically and in the way we think about it. It loses some of its mystery and luster. So we look again for something to satisfy our discontent, never admitting to ourselves that all phenomena are subject to impermanence; nothing is excluded.

If we look closely, we will see that while we're busy attaching ourselves to something, it's changing into something that we might not want or even recognize. While we obsess about a good-looking acquaintance, he or she might be turning into someone we wouldn't want to know. While we sweat about the prospect of a fashionable new outfit, current fashion makes it look outdated.

Things break, they grow old, they change their fickle minds. Sometimes they stay the same for a while, but during that time our own taste changes, the lighting changes, and in the end, we no longer want what we once did. Then we've wasted all that time and neglected other facets of our lives, all for what? For something that we don't even want anymore. The nature of the world we perceive around us is ever shifting. Any attempts to grasp things or make things permanent in an impermanent world will only frustrate us and cause needless suffering.

Sometimes we flat out deny that the object of our obsession or the cause of our discontent has changed at all, despite obvious evidence to the contrary. Instead of checking in with reality every once in a while, we hang on to a long-formed image in our minds. When we feel sadness and regret about the person who broke our heart in high school, we're stubbornly seeing an image of what was. Chances are, one or two things have changed since then. Chances are, we're beating ourselves up over something that no longer exists. If we don't watch out, we can pull this trick even when a person or object is right in front of us.

Hannah's mom looks at her adult daughter and all she perceives before her is a child just getting her first tooth.

She feels she must constantly offer Hannah advice because she can't imagine her child has changed so much that she is now able to be self-sufficient.

Otto has shown up at the same job every day for years now, but in that time his responsibilities have changed so slowly he didn't even notice. As his work became less and less creative, without friends and family around to add dimension to his life, he began to feel unfulfilled. He could tell he was unhappy, but until he acknowledged that the situation in his workplace had changed, he continued to show up to work out of habit. The fact that he hated his life for forty to sixty hours a week was a secret he kept even from himself. If he had regularly noticed his environment, he wouldn't be surprised to find himself in the position he's in, or perhaps he could have avoided it altogether.

Sometimes we try to hold on to an object or situation because we are afraid to take action. We need to acknowledge that every second we hold on, we *are* taking action. We are choosing to refuse growth, choosing to decay. There is no avoiding change or action and no point pretending either of them doesn't exist.

Another way to diminish discontent is to recognize all the ways *we* are also impermanent and subject to change. Think about it for a minute: what exactly is change? We have always treated change like something outside of us, something foreign. We view it as either a threat—something to be guarded against because we like things just the way they are—or a tool—something to use to nudge things a little bit closer to how we'd like them to be. The truth of the matter is, change is not only inevitable, it is ubiquitous, even in our own bodies. Every day, billions of cells are born and die. Some white blood cells have a life span of only a few minutes. Cells in the intestines shed once or twice a week; skin cells live for less than a month. We can't even sit perfectly still. We are always moving. Breathing. Digesting. Our hearts are beating. All this contributes to keeping the great engine of change in motion.

Otto once believed his independence was the most important thing to him, and he made great sacrifices to ensure it wasn't threatened. Now he has begun to examine his priorities. After living a lonely, isolated life, he wonders if he still wants what he once did. His ideas of independence haven't changed, but as he recognizes the many ways impermanence is part of his life, he can see that his own values have changed. Now he can try to better align his reality with his desires.

THE BACKDOOR APPROACH: IMPERMANENCE

Let go of your beliefs that any situation or circumstance is permanent. As long as you are alive, it is never too late to change your world, your situation, and most important, your outlook. In fact, if you are going to fully realize the perfection of impermanence, it is your responsibility to change your outlook as often as the world around you changes. That means constantly. Regularly check in with your surroundings and honestly admit to yourself what you see there. Watch the world transform minute-by-minute, hour-by-hour. Be open to this constant alteration. The only thing that is permanent is change.

Step Two: OPEN yourself to change.

Now it's time to make a list of changes. In one column, make a list of things that you feel are unsatisfactory about your situation. Next to each item draw an arrow pointing to the next column, the direction in which you aim to transform your situation. A list could look something like this:

Situation	Transformation
an old, broken car	a new, reliable car
an unsatisfying personal life	a loving relationship
a dead-end job	a rewarding financial opportunity
a limited understanding	enlightened understanding

This is more than just a wish list; it's a game plan. Writing it out like this helps you to see that in order to get something new in your life, you have to let go of something old—even if it's just an outdated idea or destructive habit. It could be that old patterns are incompatible with your new goals and are holding you back. When you create a list of changes, you dedicate space in your life for your dreams to take root and grow.

Examine your feelings and mentally prepare for the changes ahead. Experiment by making small alterations in your habits and environment. Once you gather some momentum, it will become easier and easier to transform your life.

Visualize: Make yourself comfortable and close your eyes. Begin by taking a deep, cleansing breath; relax your body and mind. Imagine yourself standing on the shore of an endless white sand beach. Smell the salt air, hear the sound of the waves, and feel the sun and wind on your face and your bare feet in the sand.

Gaze into the unbroken string of waves, flowing gently in and out on the shore and breaking upon nearby rocks. Watch the clouds go by and clearly see the changes and movement of the clouds. Relax and let go of any resistance to the changes. Just generate this feeling of appreciation and let yourself enjoy the total impermanent nature of your surroundings.

BENEFITS

Life is impermanent. Don't take a moment of it for granted. If you knew you had only one hour to spend with your beloved, how much of that hour would you spend fighting? How much of that time would you spend rearranging your closet? Watching TV? Any of it? You will spend almost a third of your life sleeping. Take a moment and calculate how much time you can reasonably expect to have left in this life, and then think very hard about how you can best spend your limited time to have the kind of life you want. Do you want to spend it worrying about trivial matters or suffering unnecessarily?

The benefits of recognizing the perfection of impermanence is liberation from the problems and struggles associated with discontent.

If you want to lose weight, learn to recognize change in your body. Before you eat, ask yourself, Am I hungry? or am I just eating out of habit? When you take the first bite, ask yourself, Does this taste good? Am I eating this to provide healthy energy for my body, or for some other reason? And what is that reason? As you are eating, recognize the change in your body. Do you stop when you are no longer hungry, or do you keep eating? Can you recognize when enough is enough?

If you want to improve your situation by bringing more wealth, happiness, health, peace, or love into your life, begin by inviting in change. If your house is cluttered, look around and see how many things you have accumulated that you will never use. Maybe they are things that other people have given to you, or maybe you bought them yourself. It doesn't matter. If they are cramping your life, why are you holding on to them? Out of greed? Laziness? Take an honest look at everything you own. Does it exist in front of you the way it exists in your mind, or is it broken, an outdated technology, or impractical? If so, then recycle the item. Go through your cabinets. Throw away old food that you will never eat. Give away old clothes that you will never wear. In the future, think carefully before you agree to bring any item into your home. Be open and leave plenty of room for change in your life.

If you feel insecure, recognize this as discontent. Insecurity is the mistaken belief that others have somehow achieved a permanent, more desirable state than you have, and somehow your undesirable condition is also permanent.

You are free to change your situation—and more important, your mind—as often as you like. Circumstances are always in a state of flux. Fortune is like the ocean, sometimes the tide is high; sometimes you can't even see the waves from the shore. But the tide always comes back in, doesn't it? When conditions are at their worst, you'll find treasures in the sand that were previously out of your reach.

If you aren't satisfied with what you have, take an honest look at your discontent. What is the real reason that you aren't happy with your possessions? Is it truly because what you have is unacceptable or inoperable? Then, by all means, make the changes in your life to remedy the situation and get what you need for your survival and to function in the world. But chances are, there are different reasons for your discontent. Maybe you are trying to impress other people, or maybe it's possible that you are trying to impress yourself. Either way, keep in mind that the most impressive people are the ones who live with purpose and contentment, who always do the best they can, no matter what the situation.

Anxiety and nervousness are simply symptoms of resisting change. What are you afraid of? That your new situation will be less desirable than your current one? Off the top of your head, what exactly *is* so great about your situation? What are you afraid to lose? Then take a closer look. Maybe you have outgrown your current situation and are uncomfortable admitting it to yourself or your loved ones. Maybe you are ready for a whole new world of opportunity, and it is time to admit it.

Boredom is also the product of resisting impermanence. Take a few moments and watch the world whiz by at the speed of change. If you participate willingly in any of it, it will change your life, and you'll never have time to be bored again. So what's holding you back? Don't make excuses. Instead, ask yourself if you really want what you think you want. Is it truly impossible to acquire, or are you just lazy? If you aren't lazy, then take another look at your discontent and ask why you want what you know you can't have. Don't be embarrassed that you aren't supremely successful in everything you attempt. Life is a struggle. You'll be more successful than most people if you can manage to be happy.

Realizing the perfection of impermanence is recognizing that the world is like a limitless spring of enlightenment that cannot be polluted. It contains everything you need to be happy and is everywhere that you are. There is plenty for everyone. Every second offers an opportunity to enjoy life in a new way. Even the worst situations are impermanent, offering challenges and opportunities to grow. The spring never pauses or diminishes; it just continues to flow in a kaleidoscope of beauty and richness. When you embrace impermanence, the open mind and heart you cultivate become the foundation on which all subsequent realizations can be understood.

THE ESSENCE OF IMPERMANENCE

"A seeker who relies on objects and ideas to practice generosity is like someone walking in the dark; he will not see anything."

- **The Perfection of Impermanence**   The potential for everything exists everywhere in an ever-shifting, impermanent world. Richness, beauty, and complexity are only possible because of change.
- **The Backdoor Approach**

    Step Two: OPEN yourself to change.

- **Exercise**   Make a list of changes. Write down the undesirable situations in your life and how you'd like them to be transformed.
- **Benefits**   Recognizing the perfection of impermanence helps with symptoms of discontent such as
    - a weight problem
    - dissatisfaction with what you have
    - anxiety
    - boredom
- **Conclusion**   If you realize the perfection of impermanence, you can eliminate many forms of the suffering of discontentment.

Everything can be taken from a man but . . . the last
of the human freedoms—to choose one's attitude in
any given set of circumstances, to choose one's own way.
—VICTOR FRANKL

3 | The perfection of freedom

"Look who's out on a school night again," the
bartender said over the punk rock music. He
pushed a pint of dark, frothy lager across the
bar to Otto and offered him his tattooed fist.

"Cheers, Devin," Otto said, bumping Devin's
fist with his own. He was a little embarrassed to
have Hannah see that he was a regular customer at
the Roadhouse. Not that it was a bad bar. It was a
proper pub, like they might have back home—
dark and small, a single pool table in the back in
case the clientele felt sporting. The best damn
jukebox in town. That night the place was empty.

"What'll you have?" Devin asked Hannah.

"A chocolate martini and some onion rings,"
she said, trying not to stare at the many piercings
on Devin's face.

"How about a shot of vodka and a bag of potato
chips?" Devin suggested.

"I'll just have whatever Otto's having. And can

you turn that thing down?" Hannah said to Otto's chagrin, pointing to the best damn jukebox in town.

The bartender raised an eyebrow at Otto. "Yes, ma'am," he said with a careless salute and a wink.

Otto and Hannah tucked themselves into a small booth shaped like a coffin next to the dartboard.

"I thought you said the panels were too valuable to be in a bar," Otto said.

"Well, you said you could use a drink. I had to get out of that place."

"No doubt. Since this is the last panel we're probably going to get to find before we lose our jobs. Why don't we take a look, eh?"

She passed the package to Otto. "You do the honors. You earned it. Plus, I can't see a thing in here."

Otto pushed his pint aside and unwrapped a single black panel with a golden banner drawn across the top.

"The victory banner," Otto said. "The symbol of overcoming delusions on the path to enlightenment. I've been brushing up." When he saw that Hannah wasn't impressed that he had been studying, Otto read Drake's translation to Hannah by the light of the beer sign that flashed overhead.

"A seeker who relies on behavior to practice morality is like a man locked inside a fortress. His ideas hold him prisoner. A seeker who does not depend on behavior to

> *practice morality is like a man with the key to the fortress;*
> *sheltered and safe, he can come and go as he pleases. You*
> *are not imprisoned by ideas, learning, or tradition, but*
> *free to live in equilibrium. To realize enlightenment, one*
> *must recognize that the moral nature of all phenomena is*
> *freedom."*

"Is that all? Isn't there a clue to find the next panel?" Hannah asked.

"You don't want to take a minute and think about this one first?"

"I'm too tired for this right now," Hannah said.

"A clue like *this*?" Otto revealed a brittle leaf that had been wrapped up with the panel, and passed it to Hannah. "It's a leaf from a banyan tree, otherwise known as a bodhi tree."

"The tree that the Buddha sat under when he reached enlightenment?"

Otto nodded. "One and the same."

"Cool," she said, taking it carefully in her hands. She read the message painted on it, aloud, " '*Look beyond even the most intricate constructs. Freedom must be captured alive. There you will find the next verse.*' On the back is a number, eight."

"Captured alive. Wow. You Yanks are so dramatic."

"I think I'm going to have to sleep on this one," Hannah said. When Otto offered her the panel, she held up her hand. "No, if you have any energy left tonight, you should work on it. Who knows what we'll be walking into tomorrow at work."

"Will do, Hannah. You run along home to bed. I'll take care of the check here." After Hannah left, Otto slipped the package into his jacket and brought his pint up to the bar.

"How's it going, Otto?" Devin said turning his head, but not his eyes, away from an old samurai movie playing on the TV behind the bar.

"Not too bad, mate. I'll probably get fired and deported tomorrow, but other than that, I'm doing just fine."

Devin laughed. "We could always get you a job here," Devin said, setting up another round.

"I think I prefer life on this side of the bar, thanks."

"So," Devin leaned in, "what'd you do?"

"To get fired, you mean? I defaced a Buddhist sand mandala at the library."

"Oh! What on earth did you do that for?"

"You got a minute?"

"Buckets full," Devin said.

Otto told Devin how he and Hannah had found the panels by following Drake's clues and how that had led him to destroy the mandala.

"The backdoor to enlightenment," Devin said. "Now that's something I'd like to take a look at. If I'm ever going to reach enlightenment, it'll definitely have to be through some backdoor, or trapdoor, or parachute, 'cause there's no way they'd let someone like me in through the front."

As Otto took the panel out of his jacket and set it on the bar, his cell phone rang. He saw that it was Chloe calling, silenced the ringer, and spoke to Devin. "You're welcome to take a gander. I have to say, can't make heads or tails of this one."

Devin took the panel and read the translation.

"Wow. Yeah. That is so true, man. So true," Devin said and handed the loosely wrapped panel back to Otto.

"That's it?"

"What do you want me to say?"

"So you agree with . . . whatever this is saying?"

"Agree with it? I live it. Society is locked up with its ideas about how we should look and act and," he said, pointing to the jukebox, "what music we should listen to. If you don't do what they think is right, suddenly you're not a moral person. Our whole way of life is institutionalized. All of our knowledge is 'constructed.' It doesn't necessarily reflect reality; it depends on our perception, experience, and plain old habit. You have to break free of everything you've been taught, all the ideas that society force-feeds you, and decide for yourself what to think and how to act."

"And what to pierce?"

"Or tattoo." Devin laughed. "But really, there's like some unspoken agreement between us all that no one is allowed to stray too far from the norm, or you'll be labeled a freak."

"Devin, I hate to break the news to you, mate, but look in the mirror. You *are* a freak."

"No, man, I *look* like a freak. There's a difference. You cannot rely on your perception to know my true inner nature."

"I think you might be watching too many samurai movies. So you dress different because you are expressing your rejection of our culture's norms?"

"Yup."

"Come on, Devin. What about the other culture, the culture that gets tattoos and pierces parts of their . . . face, wears boots just like yours, and drives old American cars. You might be different from some people, but you dress just like all your friends. It looks to me like you are not very free of their influence."

"Touché. Guilty as charged. Only I ride the bus. But appearances are only symbols of the real issue here," Devin said.

"Which is?"

"Which is that I know if a belief or construct gives me a hassle—like my carburetor on the '68 Camaro I used to drive—"

"I knew it!" Otto shouted, pointing at him.

"I can just walk away from it, like I walked away from that car. And that's the point," Devin said.

Otto had already walked away from most of the things in his life, even before they could give him problems. Now his job, the United States, this quest for the panels—he could just as easily leave the rest behind. He took the last swig from his beer. "I could walk away from anything in my life."

"Really?" Devin challenged. "Take a good look at the beliefs that bring you here to hang out with me whenever you aren't working. The beliefs that tell you that you have to drink even though it makes you sick. Are you free from *them*? Can you just walk away from *them*, or do you want another round?"

Otto sat in silence stunned. He'd never seen himself in that light. He wasn't free at all.

"What do you say, Otto?"

Otto shook his head and collected his things. "I say you're bloody bad for business." He put a ten on the bar and walked out, promising himself he would never drink again.

"Good," Devin said to the empty room, turned the jukebox back up, and began closing up for the night.

Monday morning, Hannah arrived late for work. She hurried through the empty parking lot to the courtyard at the heart of the Philosophical Study Center's small collection of buildings. When she saw the light blue Vespa in the shade of the center's bookstore, she smiled. Bobby was in, and he always seemed to know what was going on. Her work could wait for a few more minutes.

Bobby's lean frame draped across the counter as he read a magazine and ate a croissant, his hair falling across his forehead. His handsome face lit up when he saw Hannah coming through the door.

"Where is everyone?" Hannah asked.

"Didn't you get the e-mail? The Wycombes have left us unattended. Some meeting in Burbank. Wanna go to the Ivy for a two-hour lunch? See and be seen?" Bobby said with a smile.

"Can't. I'm so far behind. Hey, did the e-mail sound mad?"

"Mad? As in 'we don't want to go to the valley,' or mad as in 'Hannah did something wrong'?"

"The latter," Hannah admitted.

"Why do you even put up with Emma's nonsense? Did you ever hear from your friend at the literary journal back east?" Bobby asked, offering Hannah his croissant. She tore off a hunk and left the rest in his hand.

"Yeah," she said. "The job is still open."

"So why don't you take it?"

"I don't like the cold?"

"Seriously, Hannah, don't you want to be a writer? That's the way you're going to learn, not by rearranging books and writing research reports about Roman gods in Flautas."

"Plautus. Flautas are like tacos. What makes you think I want to be a writer?" Hannah asked demurely.

"I don't know, maybe because you've been talking about it since third grade."

"That was when I was a kid. I have more realistic goals now."

"Like stacking books for ten dollars an hour?"

"You also make ten dollars an hour! I know; I got you this job," Hannah said.

"Nine-fifty. I'm an actor. I'm suffering for my trade. All I'm saying is don't give up on your dreams because you've decided that they're out of your reach. You have no idea what you can do until you try. Take me, for instance, I just got the lead in *Jumpers* at the Orpheum."

"That's awesome, Bobby! Really?"

"No. But I got cast as an acrobat who gets shot in the first act."

"You can do that stuff? Like flips or tumbling or whatever?"

"There are a lot of things you don't know about Bobby Patterson, darlin'. So stay tuned!"

"I guess so," Hannah said. She tore off another bite of his croissant, and headed over to open the library.

A few minutes later Hannah found herself standing next to Otto in the Art Annex. To their surprise, there was no evidence that the sand mandala had ever existed. The colored sand had been cleaned up, the Plexiglas top had been removed, and even the platform upon which the mandala had been constructed was gone.

"It must have been that old bat Granger. She's the only one who has the key," Otto said.

"Yeah, but could she lift the platform?" Hannah said a little incredulous. It just didn't add up. She went to her desk and checked her e-mail. There was the note from the Wycombes, but, unbelievably, there was no mention of the devastated mandala, no angry tone. It seemed to Hannah that they hadn't been in to see the damage and had no idea that it had occurred. Hannah exhaled twelve hours' worth of stress.

"I can't even believe this," Otto said as he read over her shoulder. "We're free! No mention about when they'll be back?"

Hannah shook her head.

"Well, who knows, who cares," Otto said. "The only thing we should be thinking about right now is this." Otto took the leaf from his pocket and set it on the desk. The black eight on the leaf stared back at them.

"The number eight. Another bookcase?" Hannah guessed. "Case eight is over here."

Otto followed her to the back wall of the library. "We'll just have to take all these books out," Otto said. "It has to be in here somewhere."

Hannah unlocked the cabinets, as an old man came in the front door. He took off his tweed cap and nodded to Hannah.

"It's the guy researching the Freemasons," she whispered. "Empty this out and look around. I'll take care of him."

She went back to her desk and took the long list of books he offered her. As she went around the library collecting them, Otto removed books from the case. The day pressed on. The old man read his books; Hannah did some research at her desk, stealing glances at Otto who was examining the case shelf by shelf. It was long after Hannah had finished her peanut butter and raspberry jam sandwich at her desk for lunch before Otto called her over. As if on cue, the old man waved good-bye to Hannah and left them alone in the library.

Otto had replaced all the books in the case and closed the cabinets. He stood there looking supremely irritated.

"Nothing?" Hannah surmised.

"Just this." Otto bent over a corroded keyhole in the woodwork of case 8. While Hannah had been eating her sandwich, he had spent his lunch hour moving books and thinking about how nice it would be to go have a drink at the Roadhouse. But he couldn't now, could he? He had promised himself he wouldn't. He flicked the lock with his finger. "It doesn't unlock the cabinets. Maybe you have the key to it on that enormous key ring of yours?"

Hannah tried key after key, but none of them worked.

There was only one key that she hadn't tried, the "access" key from Mrs. Granger. Hannah went back to her desk and took the key from the drawer. She jiggled it in the stiff lock for a moment and then it clicked. They looked at each other with surprise.

"I think that might be a very useful key you've got there, miss," Otto said. "Not a damn thing it doesn't open."

"Now what?" she asked Otto.

"I have no idea."

He put his palms flat on the bookcase and pushed hard. Nothing happened. He tried again. Nothing happened. He slapped the bookcase, frustrated.

"Let me try," Hannah said. She pushed the bookcase and released the pressure. The right side of the case popped out a few inches. Using the handle for the bottom cabinet, Hannah pulled the case toward her easily. To their surprise, where they expected to find a dark closet or a hidden compartment they opened the door to a beautiful Japanese garden.

"My God, Hannah, you found Narnia!" Otto cried, pushing his way out the door into the sun and spinning around in jest. Outside, a beautiful garden of ferns, sculpted juniper, and bamboo spread out before them, dotted with stone lanterns. A great iron bell hung at the center. A bridge crossed a small stream that flowed around the property from a waterfall. In the center was a koi pond with a tiny stone pagoda.

"This is crazy," Hannah said. "These are the Japanese

gardens you can see through the courtyard gate. I thought this was the neighbor's yard or part of the park."

"It *is* the neighbor's yard. And do you know who the neighbor was?"

"Drake!" Hannah correctly guessed.

Otto nodded.

"You can barely see the house from here. From the street, it looks like it's abandoned," Hannah said.

"Guess not," Otto said. They took a few moments to explore the garden paths, uncomfortably aware that they were trespassing. When they came to a small teahouse in a bamboo grove, they sat down on the wooden deck in the shade. Otto took the clue out of his pocket. " *'A seeker who relies on behavior to practice morality is like a man locked inside a fortress. His ideas hold him prisoner,'* " he read.

"Well, we made it out of the fortress of ideas."

"The library?" Otto asked.

"Must be. Now that we have the key we can *'come and go'* as we please. But where's the panel?"

As if to answer the question, a leaf drifted down from the sky and joined an endless collection on the ground. Otto and Hannah looked up. A banyan tree.

As Otto crawled around the base of the tree looking for a place to dig, Hannah took the leaf out of her jacket pocket. She read the writing on it again, " *'Look beyond even the most intricate constructs. Freedom must be captured alive.'* "

"There's that Yankee phrase again," Otto said from all

fours. "All prisoners must be captured alive, argghh!" he said in an accent somewhere between a Southern belle and a pirate.

"Wow," Hannah said. "You've only lived here for, what, five years? It's remarkable how you've nailed the American accent."

"You Americans have only been speaking English for a few hundred years now, and you still haven't managed to get it right."

"Ha ha," Hannah said. "I'm thinking that phrase means something else. Hold on," she said, and ran back into the library. In the pile of books the old man had left for reshelving was one with a Japanese garden on the cover. Hannah flipped through it for a moment and found what she was looking for. She brought the book out to Otto at the center of the garden.

"Shakkei," she said.

"Gesundheit," Otto responded, matter-of-factly.

Hannah handed him the book, pointing to a picture of a mountain. "In a Japanese garden, shakkei is 'borrowed scenery,' using the surrounding landscape as part of the garden."

"So?"

"So another translation of shakkei is *captured alive*. It says right here."

Otto looked impressed. " *'Look beyond even the most intricate constructs,'* " he said, understanding.

"The tree that dropped this leaf is visible from the garden, but outside the garden walls . . ." Hannah finished her thought by pointing to the horizon. The top of another banyan tree was visible beyond the waterfall.

They made their way past the waterfall to the garden wall and, with some difficulty, over it and into the park on the other side. A five-minute hike brought them to the banyan tree.

"Look," Hannah said. Entangled in the limbs of the giant tree were the remnants of Tibetan prayer flags, the reds, yellows, blues, and greens bleached by the sun.

"The victory banner prayer flags," Otto said. "It's gotta be up there."

"Well, what are you waiting for? Go get it!" Hannah said.

"Uh, uh, princess. I got the last one. Up you go."

Hannah knew there was no use arguing with him. She frowned and kicked off her shoes. "How chivalrous."

Having an older brother, Hannah considered herself an expert tree climber. She scrambled up the tree, a little surprised at how much her abilities had deteriorated in fifteen years. A minor slip resulted in a torn pant leg and a scraped knee.

"I can see it," she said. A few feet above her head a small package was tied to the tree with the ties of the prayer flag. She climbed up farther and tugged. The string disintegrated in her hand, and the package dropped nearly thirty feet to the ground. Hannah swallowed hard, suddenly aware of her dangerous position. Without the package to think about, she found herself clutching the branch she sat on, unable to move.

"You got it?" she shouted to Otto.

"Yeah, thanks," Otto called up.

"Good. Then get me down from here!" Hannah cried.

ILLUMINATING FREEDOM

Now that we have realized that change in our lives is not only possible but guaranteed, we can take the next step to creating the lives we want. It's time to ask ourselves: Are we perfectly free to change our lives?

Freedom is our greatest privilege as human beings, but if we are all so free, why do we feel so bad? Why do we feel trapped in our jobs, our relationships, and our circumstances? Why are we overwhelmed by obligations? Why do we feel restrained from achieving everything we know we can do? Held back from happiness? If we are so free, why do we suffer from addiction, obsession, and inner conflict? Why do we feel that people are judging us? Why?

Something is holding us back from happiness and achieving our full potential. What is it? The answer is as close as our own ideas.

Our ideas are like pieces of a puzzle floating around our minds. They are micro-constructs we can use to assemble whatever picture we'd like. This picture is our map of the world. We have ideas about what a family is, ideas about what success is, ideas about what we expect from ourselves. No two pieces are automatically linked together. This is something we must do ourselves.

Hannah and Otto linked together the pieces about success and about a college education, forming a belief that successful people go to college. They also linked to that an idea that they are successful individuals, forming a belief that they should go to college. That belief was strong, so they did go to college. A picture began to form.

Otto has not linked the idea of marriage to the picture of success in his mind. His parents had a miserable marriage, so to him marriage is a kind of defeat. He most likely will not consider marriage unless he changes this belief. He had not yet linked the idea about having children to success or defeat, but he would have preferred to leave that somewhere out of the way until he made up his mind. His girlfriend, Chloe, is motivating him to reach a conclusion.

You can even force pieces together that don't easily fit, so you can reach conclusions that aren't logical or popular. They're our own ideas; we're free to arrange them any way we like. For instance, Hannah loves to write. As a child, she dreamed of becoming an author. When this goal seemed out of reach, she thought it might be just as rewarding to be a librarian. Writing books and cataloging them are two very different activities—they are in no way similar, other than that they both involve touching paper—but Hannah has forced them together, hoping to find a way to make herself happy.

Each time we fit a piece of the puzzle into place, that idea forms limits and boundaries. If Otto links the pieces of success and college education in his picture, he limits the candidates that can be successful to those who have college degrees. If Hannah fits together notions about morality and ideas about refraining from lying and stealing, she will, perhaps wisely, try to limit her own behavior in ways that exclude those acts.

Each rule and boundary we create has the potential to cause us to feel the suffering of constructs, either because of how we feel when we cross boundaries or how we feel because we are confined by them. Otto swore off drinking for the rest of his life—not because he thought he would never desire a beer now and then, but because he decided that drinking was a bad idea. Once the idea to refrain from drinking is formed, if he drinks he will feel terrible. If he goes back on his promise to himself he will have crossed the line he drew in his mind, and the result will be that he'll feel angry, powerless, frustrated, or guilty. But chances are, the formation of this idea will lead him to feel bad even if he doesn't cross the line because he has placed that line between himself and something that he desires. He will be painfully aware of the line, maybe even become obsessed with it.

If Hannah sat down and really examined her deepest desires, she would see that she would like to make a living as a writer. But when she examined her habits and beliefs, she would discover that she believes that writers become successful not because of any special skills they have developed but because they are "lucky." She doesn't think she can just work hard and learn how to become a successful writer; she thinks she must be "discovered," for her talent. This belief is keeping her from taking the actions she needs to take to pursue her dream.

Hannah's friend Bobby in the bookstore has a better attitude. Even in the competitive field of acting, Bobby doesn't get lazy and fall into the belief system that he must rely on luck to be successful. Bobby is willing to make his own luck. He is always thinking about how to reach his goal. He's open to meeting new people in his line of work, even if it's just having lunch at a spot where he can "see and be seen." He's willing to take even the smallest parts just to stay active in his field and develop new skills—in his case, acrobatics—to go after his dream.

Every piece of the puzzle we lock into place is another bit of freedom forfeited. Eventually we can become imprisoned by our own ideas and decisions. Our puzzle-piece ideas come together to form a very clear picture— a barrier that separates us from a happy, enlightened existence. Don't be afraid of having ideas, even conflicting ones, since this is a sign of an enlightened mind. But be very careful which ideas, and how many, you glue down into your picture. Be selective about the limits you put on yourself. Every limitation can stifle some part of your potential.

Even with this potential for struggle and discomfort, the human mind seems to be a lot more comfortable with a comprehensive, concrete picture than with a head full of floating pieces. We seem willing to accept the mental anguish of the suffering of constructs because it gives us the illusion of stability, even if that stability is only an arbitrarily fixed hierarchy of ideas and values. However, when the ideas we create about the world and ourselves bind rather than empower us, it's time to start questioning those constructs. In our own minds, many of us live in a ghost town of abandoned and crumbling constructs. When we find ourselves restricted by an outdated thought or an idea that someone else has imposed on us, *even the ideas in this book*, we must consciously decide if we want to continue to keep such ideas in our picture or not. If not, free it up to float.

An ever-shifting worldview might make us feel a little queasy at first, but you'll get your sea legs after a while. Then the more ideas we can leave free to mix in our minds, the more accurate our view of the world can be. The fewer ideas we assign positive or negative value, the fewer struggles we'll have.

In the perfection of impermanence, we realized that

everything changes. The system of morality that we adopt to govern our behavior is no different. The time and place you live have a lot to do with how society will expect you to behave and the standards to which you will hold yourself.

We construct the rules and restraints with which we bind ourselves and then struggle violently against them. This causes a radical swing between forced purity and reactive transgression. Suppressed impulses always come to the surface one way or another. We can either pretend they don't exist and wait for them to explode uncontrolled into our lives or face our issues honestly and rationally deal with our impulses.

In the quest for realization, focusing on controlling behavior—our own or anyone else's—isn't going to get anyone anywhere. What makes us so interested in controlling other people's behavior when it does not interfere with our own lives? If we truly want to bring the qualities of enlightenment into our lives, instead of focusing on trying to make other people obey our wishes, we should focus on helping ourselves and others realize our perfect freedom.

The danger in obedience is that it trains the mind to be lazy. An obedient mind does not react and respond to change; it waits for instruction, permission. By the time an obedient mind responds, the situation has already changed. The obedient mind is always a step behind. Obedient people eventually become powerless to act on their own because they are not accustomed to exercising their own power. If they finally do get the opportunity to exercise power, the formerly obedient person can become a tyrant, demanding respect and compliance from those he or she has managed to subjugate. This is the only order they understand. We've all seen examples of this behavior somewhere, maybe a boss, a teacher, or even a parent who was obsessed with controlling behavior because they were once controlled. If we raise our children to be obedient, this is the world that we create, a world of masters and slaves.

The power in freedom is that it allows the mind to be capable. The curious mind is engaged by change, not overwhelmed. The free mind is powerful because it is energetic and confident that it can solve whatever problem it encounters. A mind full of wonder does not seek to make others struggle because it does not struggle. It does not seek to enslave others because it has no use for enslavement. It strives instead to instill hope and a spirit of exploration in others. The only order the curious mind can tolerate is a world where we are all our own masters, doing what we love to do. This is the world we create when we raise free children who are excited about learning and life.

Rules are merely constructs that we think up, that are upheld and ultimately altered by people. We need not be imprisoned by our constructs; we can be free to live in equilibrium. This is the true realization of the perfection of freedom. Enlightenment is about liberation from suffering. Obsession about behavior creates inner conflict, outer problems, and general unhappiness.

One construct that has blocked the view of enlightenment for many seekers is the popular belief that we must work very hard for valuable things. The more valuable the resource is, the harder we must work to earn it. This belief generally holds true for constructed resources, but these only have constructed values. Things with true value are usually free. With constructed things, the more complex the construct is, the more constructed value it has.

Take, for example, the Japanese garden Otto and Hannah just discovered behind the library. With its streams and waterfall, paths, koi ponds, and bridges, it obviously took someone many years and a lot of effort to design and build. But what about the trees beyond the garden? Many things grow freely in the park, and it is the home to countless birds and animals. Some people would argue that the garden has more value than the park with its wild trees because the garden was constructed, but what value could you place on freedom?

Can you think of anything more critical to our moment-to-moment survival than things like water, air, and heat? What would you pay for air? For moisture? For the sun to continue to warm our planet? They are not luxuries. They are necessities for life. You would pay whatever you had because without these things you would die. Quickly. And yet, overall, they are still free. You purchase them with your own direct effort, not with something with an assigned value, like money or credit cards. You only have to pay for constructs.

Why, then, must we pay for land and for food? Land is not a construct, but the idea of ownership is. The use of land is free, but the construct of ownership might limit your ability to exercise that freedom. Basic food can still be obtained through direct effort in some places, but our ideas about ownership and food have greatly limited those opportunities. When you are hungry, you are more likely to buy a frozen pizza from the corner grocery store than to harvest wheat, catch a fish from a local pond, or catch a rabbit from a field. The grocery store is likely the most plentiful and palatable supplier of nourishment in your city or town. But in a dire situation, you would quickly discover that the choice to secure nourishment through direct effort is still available. You might pay to fine-tune the temperature in your home, but we are not living in a fiery inferno or in a frozen wasteland, but rather a climate hospitable to human life—for free.

The poet Tagore once wrote, "We gain freedom when we have paid the full price for our right to live." That's ridiculous. We gain freedom when we gain consciousness.

Every one of us pays the price for life with each breath we take and each beat of our heart. What's this extra price he thinks we must pay?

Every one of us is born free. Oppression can limit your circumstances, but it can never affect your freedom. Your choices are your own. Your actions are your own. Even when your actions are restricted, your thoughts and ideas are your own. You are always free to think and feel however you want to think and feel. This is the realization of an enlightened mind.

THE BACKDOOR APPROACH: FREEDOM

Now that you have opened yourself up to change, it's time to do a little mental spring cleaning. The perfection of freedom is the liberation from this struggle against, or attachment to, your own constructs in any form, and the freedom to live in equanimity, without being tormented by your own mind. This is the next step in the backdoor approach.

> Step Three: RELEASE all constructs that
> stand in the way of your goal.

Take out your list of changes again. Go down the list and, one by one, ask yourself, What obstacles exist that are currently keeping your *situation* from evolving into your *transformation*? Examine potential conflicts in your beliefs and habits that might keep you from achieving your goal. If these beliefs and habits are more important to you than your goals, adjust your goals so you can achieve them without sacrificing your lifestyle. But if these beliefs and habits are restrictive, outdated, or potentially destructive, let them go and pursue your dreams unhindered.

List the obstacles that currently stand between you and your goal. You might be surprised to find that the things that hinder you, for the most part, are under your control. Usually there aren't armies, governments, and large corporations standing between you and your happiness, only your own attitudes, routines, and beliefs.

Now ask yourself what changes you can make to assert your freedom to pursue your goals, and write down solutions. Resolve to assert yourself and remove the barriers that stand between you and your aims.

Say, for instance, your car is broken down and unreliable. You'd love a new one. Maybe a lack of funds stands in your way. But you *have* money. You just usually spend it on other things. Take a good look at how you spend your money. Are there some ways you feel pressured to spend money? Lunches and happy hours with coworkers you'd rather skip? Cable television bills you pay out of habit even though you wish you watched less TV? Expensive clothes that you don't really enjoy? Estimate how much money you waste every month doing things you'd rather not do. Whether it's wasted money, time, or energy, take back the freedom that is yours and apply your resources to live the life you want to live.

Visualize: Make yourself comfortable and close your eyes. Begin by taking a deep, cleansing breath. Relax your body and mind. Imagine yourself standing in a park on a Sunday afternoon. Children play in the grass; families enjoy picnic lunches on blankets. You can hear the sounds of a carousel and smell the popcorn that the vendors are selling. When a slight breeze arises, notice that your hand is full of bright ribbons. Look up and see that they are tied to a bunch of colorful balloons. Each balloon represent a construct that you'd like to let go of. One by one, identify the constructs, release your grasp on them, and watch them drift away.

BENEFITS

Now when you feel restrained, ask yourself, Who is restraining you? You will understand that you are only restrained by your own mind, and you are free to change it anytime. You don't need permission; you don't have to offer apologies. Change is always possible because you are not imprisoned by your mental constructs.

If you become overwhelmed by obligations, look at why you have them. Are they legal obligations, or are they someone else's expectations about what you should do? What beliefs do you hold that make you feel that you are required to do what other people want you to do? Understand that you are not bound by their expectations but by your own constructed beliefs. Decide whether you choose to continue to include these beliefs in your worldview.

When you feel that people are judging you, you'll see that they are judging you by the standards of some impermanent construct or another. Remember, you are always free to change your mind about the value of other people's opinions. They are free to have opinions; you are free to ignore them.

When you feel argumentative or defensive, you will remember how foolish it is to make yourself upset over an impermanent construct. If you just like to argue, practice arguing both sides of every dispute, so you don't become attached to narrow ideas or proving yourself right. Everyone has innumerable opinions and beliefs; the chances that anyone will agree with you entirely are nearly nonexistent. Accept that fact, and think about dismantling any constructs you have built about the importance of impermanent opinions and the necessity of agreement. It's entirely possible to live a happy, enlightened life without ever wholly agreeing with anyone about anything.

Are you obsessed? Do you suffer from addiction? Look at why you value the object of your obsession, beyond the obvious reasons. What does the item or substance mean to you? Once you understand, just let it go. Focusing on the substance or object in a negative way is not much different from focusing on it in a positive way. You are still indulging in obsession.

And remember, when you decide to live in a country or state, you enjoy the privilege of residency in exchange for an agreement to follow the laws of the territory. If you don't agree with those laws, then it is your right to work to have the laws changed or to leave and find a place that better suits your inclinations. You are always free to break a law, but you will cross a line in your mind and cause yourself some struggling. You can also reasonably expect to pay the consequences associated with your trespass.

Blind obedience is the result of brainwashing, and no one was ever brainwashed into enlightenment. You cannot even follow orders into enlightenment. Realization is not a military drill. It isn't some fort to be captured by storm. Others might be able to show you the spots where you're getting hung up, but every step of the way you need to make up your own mind. The only steps that count are the ones you take yourself.

Realizing the perfection of freedom is recognizing that your constructs only have the power that you give them. You are perfectly free to interact with the world in any way that you choose. You create your own limits; you make your own rules. Your own constructs are the only things that can stand between you and enlightenment. Like the wandering nomad who ignored the walls and barriers, you can choose to walk right past your constructs, even, and especially, if they have been in place for thousands of years, since things are constantly in flux. No rituals, incantations, or special permissions are required to experience the world without constructs. How can any finite construct limit that which is infinite?

THE ESSENCE OF FREEDOM

*"A seeker who relies on behavior to practice
morality is like a man locked in a fortress.
His ideas hold him prisoner."*

- **The Perfection of Freedom**   We are not imprisoned by our constructs, or forced to create rules to struggle against, but free to live in equilibrium.
- **The Backdoor Approach**
  Step Three: RELEASE all constructs that stand in the way of your goal.
- **Exercise**   Put your goals in writing, and examine potential conflicts in your beliefs and habits that might keep you from achieving your goals.
- **Benefits**   Recognizing the perfection of freedom also solves problems with constructs such as feeling
  - restrained and judged
  - argumentative, defensive
  - obsessed, suffering from addiction
  - overwhelmed by obligations, inner conflict
- **Conclusion**   We are at liberty to remain in equilibrium if we choose, rather than exist in the bondage of imposed reaction. Our constructs have only the power that we give them.

Happy the man who has been able to learn the
cause of things.

—VIRGIL

"I can't believe I have to go back to work looking
like this," Hannah said, sitting on the ground under
the tree, examining her state. "I have leaves in my
hair." Her pants were also ripped, her knee was
bleeding, and her shirt was stained with grass.

"Yes, but they're bodhi leaves," Otto pointed out.

"You were supposed to catch me."

"I tried. But there's no use in both of us getting
hurt." He unwrapped the panel from the paper and
plastic. "Oh, this is pretty. There's an umbrella at
the top. You could've used that to come down off
that tree like Mary Poppins."

"Shut up, Otto," Hannah said.

"Okay, okay. Why don't you do the honors," he
said, and handed the panel to her. "It's the least I
can do."

"That's for sure," she said and snatched the
panel from him. When she saw the golden parasol
painted across the center, she softened. "It *is* pretty."

"Told you."

She read the panel to Otto. " '*A seeker who does not rely on self-control to practice patience will wait until a tiger feeds and safely pass by while the tiger sleeps.*' "

"That's you, angry tiger falling from the treetops," Otto said.

Hannah rolled her eyes and continued to read. " '*We live in a system of cause and effect. Every action has a reaction. To realize enlightenment, one must recognize that true patience is understanding the perfection of causality.*' "

"Causality?"

"That's what it says," Hannah said.

"Well, that's easy enough. Common sense, like. What does the clue say?"

" '*Recognize that the effects of actions are varied, endless, and often unexpected. Follow the chain of the effects of your actions to the next verse.*' "

"That sounds like an excellent project for *after* work," Otto said.

"Yeah," Hannah agreed, "I've got to get back and re-open the library. Meet me in the parking lot after dinner? Say eight?"

"Or meet me in the parking lot for dinner, say eight?"

Hannah considered his proposal, and his odd looks. She frowned.

"You'll want to clean yourself up a bit, though," Otto added when he saw the reluctance in her face. "I've got a reputation in this country."

Hannah smiled and caved in to the spontaneity of it all. "Okay," she agreed. It's a date; she completed the thought in her mind, but kept the words from reaching her lips.

When Hannah got back to the library, there was a message for her on her desk. She dropped the panel and the garden book and dialed the number immediately.

"Mom, is everything okay with Dad?"

"Yes," her mom answered, sounding better than Hannah expected. "But if he would have taken care of himself all these years, we wouldn't even be having this discussion. Just hold on, I'll let your father tell you." There was a brief pause on the phone line as Hannah's mom passed the phone to her father. Hannah sighed, relieved that she wasn't calling home to hear bad news.

"I don't know what's wrong with your mother," her father started. "After our talk the other day, I've finally decided to let Dr. Harris have a shot at these old arteries of mine."

"Daddy, that's great!" Hannah said. "I thought that's what she wanted."

"She's just scared. The operation isn't without risks, but if I want to make up for lost time with you kids, I have to do something."

"When are you going in?"

"Tomorrow."

Hannah was shocked. She began to feel some of the fear and anger her mother was experiencing. "Wow, that was fast," she said.

"Your daddy doesn't mess around. Now," he said in a conspiratorial tone, "did you find any more of those enlightenment panels?"

"Two. We just pulled one down from a tree a few minutes ago," Hannah said.

"Then tell me all about it, Kitten."

That night Otto waited in the parking lot for Hannah. He didn't have a car, so he figured they could walk over to the Derby and get a quick bite to eat. He was early, so he pulled out his cell phone and dialed up Chloe. He had done a lot of thinking since his discussion with Devin. If he had been wrong about drinking, maybe he was wrong about other things, too. He always thought that to be free he had to run away, but now he wondered if that wasn't just another one of his bad ideas. Maybe freedom was about not having to run, about being open to experiencing anything.

Chloe answered on the third ring. "Oh, Otto," she said when she heard his voice. "Can I get back to you? I'm just on my way out." Her voice was flat. He had to wonder if she was just putting him off the way he had done to her so often since he had come back from his holiday with her.

"I wanted to talk to you," he said.

"Well, Ruari was just taking me to Inverness to pick up some things for the baby's room. Maybe you could call back some other time."

"Will do," he said into the phone. Ruari. His best mate. "Some other time."

"You all done?" Hannah said from behind him. Otto turned around and counted himself lucky. Hannah looked lovely in a black linen sundress, her hair swept up casually.

"Quite done," Otto said snapping his phone closed. "Now let's see who's playing at the Derby."

Live swing music and burgers went a long way to take Otto and Hannah's minds off the stresses of the day. Otto's easy manner helped Hannah relax about her father's condition, and Hannah's pretty face helped keep Chloe's outing with Ruari off Otto's mind.

"You wanna dance?" Hannah shouted across the dark booth to Otto when they had finished their burgers.

"Scottish men don't dance sober, and I've sworn off the hard stuff, so you, my lady, are flat out of luck. You know," Otto said, "we don't have to turn these panels over to Emma."

"You think we should hide them again?" Hannah asked.

"Ah no. That's not what I'm saying."

"What are you saying, Otto? That we should steal them?"

"It's not stealing if no one knows they're missing. I looked online last night. Do you know what a manuscript like this would sell for at auction? I have a friend at Sotheby's. Why don't we send him some pictures?"

Hannah just stared at him. "So what was all that talk about Drake and how important the collection is? I never told you this, but when Emma locked the illuminated manuscript up in the vault, I caught a glimpse of what was inside. Do you know what's in there?"

"It must be amazing, all those old books."

"No, Otto, there's hardly anything in there. Most of them are gone. Stolen. And you're no better than the Wycombes. You're just looking to make a buck."

Otto took a moment to process the fact that the vault was nearly empty, and then he refocused on the conversation at hand. "No. That's not what I'm saying. Drake was great. I wish he were still around. I have a million things I'd like to talk to him about. But the money we could make off this thing could set us both up for life."

"If that's what you want to do, then count me out," Hannah said. "I should have known it would come to this."

"No, Hannah. Okay, look. Just forget I ever said anything. I was only asking."

"Well, the answer is no."

"I won't mention it again," Otto said. Hannah frowned. Otto put two twenties on the table and led her out of the noisy restaurant by the hand.

"Close your eyes," he said when they got outside.

"Why?"

"Because I've got something really really special lined up for you to make up for my unwillingness to make an arse out of myself for you on the dance floor. Come on. Close your eyes."

Hannah did. Otto spun her around three times, put her hand on his shoulder, and covered it with his own. "Now follow me," he said.

They slowly made their way down the street, Otto leading Hannah blindly. After a minute of walking in silence Otto stopped.

"Can I open my eyes now?" Hannah asked.

"Almost," he said. "Sit down."

Hannah tried to sit on something bench-height, but there was nothing there.

"Lower," Otto said.

Hannah lowered herself further. It was a curb. She was sitting in a parking lot.

"Wait here one second. I'll be right back," Otto said.

After what seemed like ages, Otto returned.

"Okay, open your eyes."

Hannah did. She was sitting under a bright red neon sign. "Thrifty drugstore?"

"Aye." He pulled two ice cream cones from behind his back. "Fifty-cent cones. Chocolate?"

"Sure," Hannah said.

He gave Hannah a hand up onto a retaining wall. "It's only a short walk through the park to the tree where we found the panel," he said.

"You know," she said as they walked together, "when I

was a kid, my dad used to buy me ice cream cones there and then take me up to the observatory to look at the stars. I might never get the opportunity to do that again."

"Is he sick?"

Hannah nodded. There were tears in her eyes. Otto stopped walking.

"I'm so sorry," he said, and leaned against a tree. "You want to forget all this enlightenment panel stuff and go up to the observatory right now? We'll go watch a Pink Floyd laser show or something and name a planet after your dad." Hannah covered her face. Otto tossed the rest of his ice cream into the bushes.

"Come here," he said. He took her in his arms and kissed her softly on the cheek, catching a tear. He didn't say anything. She turned her head slightly, and he kissed her on the lips. They both felt a little shocked at what they'd done.

"Now that's all you're getting out of me until you cheer up. I usually try to avoid soggy lassies." Before she could protest, her eyes caught sight of something on the ground. "What's this?" she said, wiping the last of her tears from her eyes. She knelt on the ground and swept away some of the leaves that had collected beneath the tree.

"Is this the tree from this afternoon? The bodhi tree?"

"You think I stopped here just to kiss you? Of course it is."

Otto shined a small flashlight along the ground where Hannah revealed a string running down from the tree into the leaves below.

"It's connected to the prayer flags. It must have gotten pulled up when I ripped the package out of the tree." She pulled on the string and it came easily from the ground.

"It's leads away," she said, "back to the garden."

Tentatively, they pulled on the string and followed, pulled and followed, all the way back to a small gate in the garden wall. A pair of terrifying statues stood guard.

"We must have missed this gate before. What are these creepy things?" Otto asked.

"They're Fu dogs. Guardian statues. Tibetans call them snow lions. To keep out people with bad intentions."

"How can they keep anything out? They're statues."

"If you pass between them without wearing red, they curse you."

"That's nonsense," Otto said, but he didn't go through the gate.

They could hear the rushing of the waterfall in the garden just on the other side. Hannah pulled the string again and this time it stuck somewhere on the other side of the wall. Otto shone his dim pinpoint of light into the darkness.

"Pull again. Harder," he said.

Hannah did.

"It's stuck on something," she said.

Otto took the string out of her hand and yanked it hard. Simultaneously, the string came loose in his hand and it grew uncannily quiet. They both cautiously walked on the uneven ground through the gate, to investigate the sudden quiet. Their jaws dropped at what they saw. The once thunderous waterfall was tapering down to a slow leak.

"It's like someone shut the waterfall off," Otto said.

"It's *just* like that, you idiot. You must have shut the pump off when you pulled that string!" Hannah exclaimed.

They watched in horror as the last of the water drained from the upper basin of the waterfall. Water lilies slumped in the muck and a small turtle stared back at them, amazed suddenly to be on dry land.

"Now what?" Hannah asked

"Now," Otto said, climbing down into the basin, sinking deep in the mud, "I'm going to bring this poor turtle down to the lower pond, go home, and go to bed. I think I've done enough damage for one night." He picked the turtle up. When he tried to stand again, he slipped, slamming his head on a slimy rock. Damn curse, he thought.

It was there in that position that he noticed some pale letters glowing through the pond scum on the walls of the basin. He wiped away the scum with his forearm, and fumbled for his flashlight.

"If you're looking for more wildlife to rescue . . ." Hannah started.

"I found something."

Hannah jumped down beside him, cringing as the mud swallowed her feet and shoes.

"It's Drake's handwriting. *'Light the third lamp to illuminate the path to enlightenment.'* "

"Oh I know this one," Otto said. "It's a reference to the philosopher Atisha. *The Lamp for the Path to Enlightenment.* He wrote it in the eleventh century."

"Or it could be a reference to the lamps right over there," Hannah reasoned.

Sure enough, next to the words an arrow pointed across the garden to three low Japanese stone lanterns.

"It's funny," Hannah added, "how you overthink things until they make no sense whatsoever, or you don't think at all," she motioned to the emptied waterfall.

"It's funny how you're a cheeky, cheeky bird. Hold my turtle."

He handed her the turtle and climbed out of the basin. They snuck quietly across the garden. Otto deposited the turtle in the koi pond where it disappeared beneath the water with a few bubbles, and they went to examine the lantern. Otto handed Hannah a match.

"Your turn."

Hannah exhaled. As she struck the match, Otto shone his small light around the garden. Something caught his eye.

As she lit the lantern, Otto cried out, "No, Hannah!"

He rushed over to knock the match from her hand.

He bent over and tried to blow out the lantern, but he was too late. The flame disappeared up into the lantern beyond the reach of his breath.

"What are you doing?" Hannah said.

Otto pointed to a taut line running from the lantern into the darkness. As he did so, the flames within the lantern burned through the line, releasing it. The line went slack. Instantly, the big iron bell at the center of the garden began to clang and the lights in Drake's old house went on. Hannah covered her ears and ducked down. Otto dove over the lantern and caught the string. He pulled it tight again. The bell's clapper slammed against the side one last time and then the bell finally went silent.

Otto lay flat on the ground, and Hannah crouched in the bushes as the front door to Drake's old house swung open, and Emma Wycombe stepped out into the night air angrily clutching her bathrobe around herself. She scanned the garden looking for intruders. After the longest two and a half minutes of their lives, Emma went back inside and turned off the light.

"Oh this is just great," Otto whispered when the house grew dark. "This is the Wycombes' house now? The panel is in there?"

"The lamp didn't illuminate anything; it rang a bell!" Hannah exclaimed. "That's not fair. What are you doing?"

Otto still lay on the ground clutching the string.

"If I let it go, the bell will start ringing again. And then——" Otto started.

"And then the porch light will go on again."

"Among other things. That nasty old cow will come out here and catch us, and cook us for dinner with chow mein noodles."

"It's too late for dinner. You're not listening to me."

"That's because I've gone bloody deaf from that bloody bell. Stop smiling! I've got a cramp in my arm!"

"The clue said lighting the lamp will illuminate where the panel is hidden. When I lit the lantern, it rang the bell, causing that porch light to go on. The light points over there somewhere."

"Where?" Otto said.

"I don't know," Hannah admitted. "I wasn't paying attention."

Just then Otto's phone rang. Digital tones playing "The Flower of Scotland" sounded flatly from his pocket. His hands, however, were occupied.

"Get it!" Otto whispered loudly. Hannah dove over and patted him down until she could find the source of the noise. She found the phone and pressed the button on the side to silence it.

"You have one missed call," Hannah giggled.

"Thanks."

She looked at the phone again. "Who's Chloe?"

The look on Otto's face didn't tell her everything about Otto's situation with Chloe, but it told her enough.

"You *are* an arse."

"I'm sorry," Otto said contritely from the ground.

"Don't, Otto. Forget about it," Hannah said.

"You want to find this next panel now?" Otto asked.

Hannah nodded without looking at him.

"Well, there's only one way to find out where it is. We've got to get that light to turn on again."

Hannah turned back to him, "Okay. Do it."

Otto released the string. The bell rang out, the porch light went on, and they saw exactly where the clue was hidden.

"What the hell are you two doing in my garden?"

They turned to see Emma standing behind them.

Before they could answer she continued, "What are you doing out here?"

"We didn't know this was your house, I swear," Hannah blurted out. She looked up and saw there was a light on in the upstairs window. Someone was watching them through the shutters.

"And that makes it all right to stalk around in the middle of the night vandalizing my garden? I guessed that was what you were doing with the sand mandala, and now I'm sure. While I think about what I'm going to do with you, I'm going to have to ask that you return the keys to the library. I don't trust you."

Hannah and Otto both thought about their chances of finding the rest of the panels without the keys. It didn't look good.

"Now wait, Emma," Otto started.

"Give me the keys." Emma shook her head at them in disgust. "After your actions lately, what did you both expect?"

ILLUMINATING CAUSALITY

Why is the world so angry? At home there is domestic abuse. On the highways there is road rage. In our schools we have bullies and the violence that boils over in response to them. We murder each other. We fight wars. The popular media is full of violent images and sentiments. The evidence is everywhere: We are frustrated.

And what about you? Are you irritated? Do you get road rage? Do you have a temper? Hold a grudge? Do you ever feel hopeless? Are you sometimes inclined to indulge in magical thinking or belief in superstition? What do all these feeling have in common and what causes them?

We don't feel angry when we are in control of a situation. Anger is not an expression of the strong. It is caused by feelings of impotence. Despite our most sincere efforts, we watch every day as our actions are thwarted and our desires denied us. We try and do not succeed. We are often left baffled and discouraged.

Now, more than ever, our problems are drawn on a much larger scale: With a global community come global-sized problems. We can get along with our neighbors, but how are we supposed to live peacefully with those who seem utterly different from us? We can balance our own checkbooks, but how are we supposed to end poverty? We can keep our house clean, but what about the environment? Whether we realize it or not, we want things to run smoothly. We want everybody to be happy, but solutions to big problems don't come easily, and we are left feeling small, ineffectual, and invalid.

The natural energetic response to feelings of impotence on any scale is anger. Refusing to submit to defeat, anger is a desperate attempt to try anything to change an undesirable situation. When you use anger and violence as a tool, you have no control of the outcome, but you are pretty much guaranteed that something will change. Problem is, it usually changes for the worse.

Hopelessness is the lazy man's anger. Rather than respond to frustration with action, the hopeless person skips right ahead to defeat. An angry person's chances of inducing positive change are very slim, but a hopeless person has no chance at all.

So how can we respond to frustration? How can we get things to go our way? How can we move beyond the confusion, avoiding the pitfalls of anger and hopelessness, to overcome our feelings of ineffectuality and invalidity?

Once we realize that we are free to act appropriately in any situation, regardless of the past or present opinions of others and illusory constructs, we also realize that we are also perfectly responsible for the consequences of our actions. Instead of begrudgingly accepting a situation we cannot control, we should seek to understand the scope of the influence of our actions.

To relieve feelings of powerlessness, we don't require patience; we just need to understand actions and what we can reasonably expect from them.

Actions are part of an organized system, in which one action leads to many consequences, which create more actions. When Otto and Hannah first began looking for the *Backdoor to Enlightenment* panels, they started a chain of reactions. Not only did their discovery lead them to destroy the sand mandala in the library and sneak into the Wycombes' garden, but it also led Hannah to help change the course of her father's life, Otto to stop drinking, and both of them to reconsider the directions their lives were taking. As you see, the consequences of finding that first panel went on and on.

Causality is the relationship that links the actions of cause and effect. It is the operating system of change, and the force that churns existence. Every action is an effect that is preceded by a cause. This doesn't mean that causality is linear, like a line of dominoes; rather it is highly complex and multidimensional, like the swelling and mixing of the ocean.

There is evidence of the system of cause and effect all around us. We intuitively employ it to survive and achieve our goals. When we are hungry, we don't hit an apple with a hammer. We eat it. When we want to go somewhere, we don't click our heels together three times. We get in a vehicle and shorten the distance between our destination and us until we are there. When we need to solve a math problem, we work it out step-by-step, through methods that we have learned by trial and error. We don't write down random numbers until one looks good.

Every action has innumerable consequences, many of which are not apparent to the naked eye. Even when you think you aren't doing anything, you are breathing, removing oxygen from the air and replacing it with carbon dioxide. Food in your stomach goes through chemical transformation. Your body transfers heat to your environment. Your very existence changes the world every second you are alive, and then when you die, your decomposition, or cremation, will affect it, too. This cycle of action and reaction, of cause and effect, stretches on into infinity. It began before life existed and will continue long after it is gone. This is the perfection of causality.

Recognizing the link between causes and their effects and making predictions based on what we have observed in the past have made us successful thus far as a species. Yet our failure to recognize this cycle and take timely, appropriate action is possibly the greatest threat to our species. Understanding causality is important stuff.

When we say someone is reasonable, logical, or rational, we are saying that he has a habit of thinking in a way that draws conclusions from available information, that he can accurately link causes to their effects. Scientists use the established order of cause and effect to learn about the natural world. They call this the *scientific method*, a highly organized form of common sense. They observe effects in the natural world, and on the basis of these observations they formulate educated guesses, or hypotheses, about possible causes. They conduct experiments and ultimately use the findings to make predictions about the world. If you can discover the cause of an unfavorable phenomenon, you can work to eliminate it. If you can discover the cause for a favorable phenomenon, you can work to encourage it.

While data can be manipulated—and not all facts discovered are always put to good use—by recognizing causality, science has been able to apprehend and effectively respond to the knowable universe. As our understanding of the world grows more detailed and complex, we are able to define and rationally understand things we once were forced to explain only in terms of myth and mysticism. Science works to shatter the very views about a relatively static material world that it once helped create. This ability to cast off outdated ideas and question every assumption can offer us the most accurate and exciting way of describing and understanding spirituality to date.

Once you understand causality and the extent of our

interdependence, you are positioned to relieve more unnecessary suffering from your life. If the suffering of pervasive action can be likened to a wild ride on an unstoppable motorcycle with unfamiliar controls, realizing the perfection of causality is the calm that accompanies the clear understanding of the far-reaching scope of cause and effect. We can't slow down or stop the world, and we can't get off. Save your energy and stop struggling to achieve that impossibility.

But we can steer ourselves through the world by figuring out which actions will most likely bring about the effects we desire; thus we can avoid crashing into obstacles and go wherever we want. Most important, with this understanding we'll calm down enough to enjoy the ride.

After we recognize how causality works and begin to understand the scope of our influence, feelings of anger and frustration will dissipate. We are not powerless; we all have the same potential for having influence upon the world.

Actions can be physically caused or influenced by the mind. The mind can make a decision to act, for instance, but the mind itself cannot act. For that, it needs a body, a physical link, to the outside world. The mind cannot be directly affected by action, but it can be influenced by the physical world over a long time (learning) or a short time (perception). Either way, influence must be interpreted by the mind itself. Interpretation always separates the physical world from the mind. Simply put, actions create causes; the mind creates influence. The mind can be neither a cause nor the direct effect of a cause, but it is not free from influence.

It is impossible to keep our decisions cleanly beyond the effects of outside influence because we are interdependent, inseparably joined to each other and our environment by, among other things, the effects of our actions. We cannot be free from others, but we can be free from ourselves, from constructs that impair our ability to react effectively in the world. Where we direct our consciousness is a decision we make every second.

It is important to recognize the scope and limitations of our actions on ourselves and the outside world. When we want something done, we're going to have to do it ourselves, or at least create a direct link. If there is no direct link between ourselves and another thing, we cannot affect it. If there is no indirect link between ourselves and another thing, we cannot even influence it. Notice the difference between the two. Direct links lead to physical effects. Indirect links can only influence physical effects. If that influence is strong, we might be successful; if it is weak, we stand a lesser chance of success.

For example, when Otto released the string from the lantern to the bell, that physically caused the bell to ring. This was a direct link between Otto's actions and the ringing bell. The ringing bell then *influenced* Emma to stop whatever she was doing and come outside to investigate. Whether or not she chose to respond to that influence depended on her will, learning, and the strength of the appeal of the ringing bell. There was an indirect link between Otto's action and Emma's reaction. Emma's reaction depended on Otto's influence upon her mind; Otto's actions did not physically move her body.

The realization of the perfection of causality is the antidote for superstition and magical thinking. These phenomena are symptoms of a combination of feelings of helplessness and the failure to mentally link appropriate cause and effect.

Some things we think of as magic are really just the result of influence by way of suggestion. Take the Fu dogs in the story. Hannah's inaccurate but spooky account of their purpose set Otto a little on edge. When he found himself in an awkward position, he was distracted by his negative thoughts and therefore became more accident-prone. When he did finally fall, he was quick to blame it on the Fu dog curse, rather than on his own distracted mind and the circumstance of being in a slimy pond basin at midnight in slick shoes. This is an example of influence, rather than causality. We are always free to ignore suggestions. They cannot directly harm us; they can only influence us to harm ourselves.

We have come a long way from the Dark Ages when, living under the tyranny of ignorance, we attributed every illness and misfortune to the work of demons or witch-craft. Rational thought is essential to economic develop-ment, health, happiness, and enlightenment.

We don't have to believe, but we definitely have to think. When we abandon intelligent thought in favor of superstition and pseudoscience, we're heading down the road to ignorance and poverty, not the path to enlighten-ment. There is nothing mystical or supernatural about en-lightenment; it is the natural outcome of an open, clear, and rational mind. Logical thinking, observation, and the scientific method aren't perfect tools for improving our physical condition, but right now, they're the best ones we've got.

There will always be things that are unknowable to the conceptual mind. The unknown is the domain of all religions of the world, and they seem to perfectly express so many of our hopes about these things. Religion offers solace in the face of the great mysteries.

Religion is personal. Belief is personal. We have our beliefs because of the influences we have experienced in our lives. Everyone in the world has different experiences and influences. It is unlikely that one person will agree entirely with anyone else in the world; how much less likely is it that the whole world will ever agree?

Fortunately, it is entirely unnecessary that we agree about the unknowable things or argue about the know-able ones. How can we argue about anything that cannot be proved or disproved? Argument depends on evidence. Arguments about things that can be proved or disproved tend to be short. Once there is proof, there can be agreement. No matter what religion we practice, if we realize the perfection of casuality, rationality will be a language we all can speak, a peaceful country of which we can all become a citizen.

THE BACKDOOR APPROACH: CAUSALITY

Every cause has an effect; the perfection of causality is realizing the incredible extent of this truism. When you understand causality, you see clearly how the world unfolds and you can eliminate false expectations. Impatience, anxiety, and anger dissolve when you act with foresight, recognizing the natural effects of your actions. In the last chapter, you worked on minimizing obstacles and distractions that can keep you from your goal. Now take the steps required to make your dreams a reality.

Step Four: CREATE the causes that produce the effects you desire.

The best way to start is to get out another piece of paper and come up with a plan. Design a strategy of actions you can take to bridge the gap between your situation and your transformation. Begin by determining a date by which you'd like to see your dream materialize. Make a list of all the steps you'll need to take between now and then. Don't worry if some steps seem impossible for you today. The person you will be in the future who will face the task is an entirely different person, with completely different capabilities and opportunities. The most important part of this process is to organize your thoughts and break a large, seemingly difficult task into smaller, manageable goals.

Next, break out a calendar and plot out smaller goals to help you stay on track. Include things like making contacts and celebrating when you complete your mini-objectives. Put this calendar somewhere you can refer to it and update it regularly. You will be amazed how things will go exactly as planned.

For example, if you really want to transform your dead-end job into a better opportunity, you should begin by setting a target date by which you hope to be out of your current situation. Of course, you might be able to beat your target date, but having a target date will help you keep a positive attitude, realizing that the end is, at least, in sight. Next, list the steps you have to take to get a new job. You need to update your résumé, talk to some friends to scout out job openings, and maybe try a placement service. Plot all of these goals on a calendar, leaving time for interviews and callback interviews. Success is a numbers game: the more résumés you get out in circulation, the more chance you have at finding a new job quickly. The more options you secure, the more chance you have at landing an opportunity you will be satisfied with. Once you complete your planning, you can get to work and transform your situation.

Visualize: Make yourself comfortable and close your eyes. Begin by taking a deep, cleansing breath; relax your body and mind. Take another deep breath and imagine yourself smiling and walking in a beautiful garden; smell the fresh fragrances as your bare feet touch smooth green grass. Now imagine gazing into the vivid color of each plant and flower in the garden. Feel your skin under the warm sun and the cold breeze of the wind. Take another deep breath and imagine yourself picking up leaves and dry flowers in your garden. Rearrange the rocks on the bank. See the full blooms filled with butterflies. Listen to the sound of the waterfall within the pond. While you enjoy the garden, let your body and mind be swept away into this safe, beautiful landscape.

Now with that image in your mind, ask yourself what you want to create in your life. Respond and visualize what you want with the same clarity with which you visualized your garden. Imagine what it would look and feel like to fulfill your goals. Think of smells and tastes associated with your goals.

Each wish is the beginning of some creation. Let your desire guide your actions to affect your life. Now gently open your eyes and embrace your life with creative attitude.

BENEFITS

Realizing the perfection of causality is the antidote for anger and frustration because it enables you to understand the range of your actions and influence. If in your previous attempts you failed either to make a direct causal link or to use the appropriate force of influence, you can adjust your methods and try again. If you realize that you do not possess the appropriate physical or influential force, you can either work to build it or recognize that the target is beyond your reach. Remember, anger and frustration stem from feelings of powerlessness. Things irk us because we know that they are possible, even if they are denied to us for some reason. Realizing the perfection of causality, you will learn to recognize the difference between impossibilities and difficulties and eliminate frustration and anger.

Do you hold a grudge? When you understand causality, you will see that holding a grudge only creates negative effects for yourself. If you have truly been wronged, your opponent will have to experience the negative effects of his actions. It is not necessary for you to do anything extra. Don't add yourself to the list of people who must suffer for his crime by committing one of your own. Harboring negative feelings only disturbs your happiness. You don't have to agree with what was done, but let go of the anger and resentment. Move on with your life. Your equilibrium in the present is the most important objective. Don't lose sight of that. You can't live an enlightened existence if you are obsessed with the past.

Do your best to minimize the suffering you cause yourself and others, but don't dwell on suffering that you don't directly cause, lest you create more problems for yourself.

When you realize the perfection of causality, you will clearly perceive the link between the causes and effects of your actions. If you are thirsty, you should drink.

THE ESSENCE OF CAUSALITY

*"A seeker who does not rely on self-control to
practice patience will wait until a tiger feeds
and safely pass by while the tiger sleeps."*

- **The Perfection of Causality**   We live in an action/
reaction system of causality, and every action has
a reaction.
- **The Backdoor Approach**
   Step Four: CREATE the causes that will produce
   the effects you desire.
- **Exercise**   Plan your goals on a calendar. Plot the
actions you will take. Cut out pictures. Involve all
your senses.
- **Benefits**   Recognizing the perfection of causality also
solves problems stemming from pervasive action,
such as
  - anger
  - frustration
  - holding grudges
  - hopelessness
- **Conclusion**   Recognize the scope of your actions and
expect their effects.

Whoever said anybody has a right to give up?

—MARIAN WRIGHT EDELMAN

5 | The perfection of intent

"Now go home. If anything like this happens again,
I won't hesitate to call the police," Emma Wycombe said finally after she had lectured Hannah
and Otto thoroughly on their behavior of late.

Emma retied her bathrobe definitively and
marched back inside, closing the door behind her.
Hannah and Otto stood in the garden, still shocked
by the outcome of their actions. After a moment
they heard a pump switch on and water began to
rush again into the upper basin of the waterfall. Then
the lights of the big brick house switched off, leaving them in the dark garden feeling like thieves.

"Well that's just grand. We're never going to be
able to find the rest of the panels if we don't have
the . . ."

Hannah dangled the key labeled "access" before
Otto's eyes as if to hypnotize him. It worked. "I
slipped it off the ring before I gave the keys to
Emma," she explained.

"Sneaky, sneaky. I could kiss you!" Otto said.

"Not unless you feel like being slapped," Hannah replied.

"Okay, okay. Touchy."

"Let's just get what we came for and get out of here. The light shone on that stepping-stone over there. The panel must be under it. I don't care whose turn it is. Go get it," Hannah said.

Otto didn't argue. Terrified, he crept over to the large slate stone. Before he turned it over, he noticed the familiar shape of the parasol etched into the rock. As quickly as he could, he flipped over the stone, snatched the package out from beneath it, and darted back into the bushes.

"I'm willing to bet you don't want to come to my place to unwrap this. You think that access key opens my office?" Otto asked.

Hannah and Otto weren't surprised when, as they stood at the top of the stairs in the night air in front of his office door, the key turned easily in the lock.

"This is where you work?" Hannah asked. She surveyed Otto's badly lit office. It was the size of a watchmaker's, stuffed with boxes of paper, printers, and computers. Otto went to his desk and quickly turned over a business card and a stack of printouts before Hannah could see what they were.

"It's freezing in here," Hannah said, wishing she had a sweater.

"Nah," Otto said. "It's the temperature of a Scottish isle in the dead of summer."

"Which isle?" Hannah asked, catching the nostalgia in his voice.

"Skye," Otto admitted.

"Is that where you grew up?" Hannah asked.

Otto nodded. "Across the Kyle Rhea in a little town called Glenelg."

"Is that where Chloe is?"

Otto tilted his head in affirmation without looking at her.

Hannah noticed a chart on the wall. "I'm not prying, but why do you have the tidal charts of eastern Canada hanging on your wall?" Hannah asked.

"Do you want to look at this thing or not?" Otto said and began unwrapping it. Inside the layers of plastic and paper was another black panel, this one embellished with an endless golden knot.

" *'A seeker who does not rely on actions to practice virtuous effort knows there is no point pushing a boulder up an endless hill; he will never reach the end of his endeavor. The boulder can easily be moved in his mind,'* " Otto read. " *'Just as actions have no beginning or end, neither does intent. To realize enlightenment, one must recognize that the perfection of intent shapes worlds.'* "

"Here's the clue," he said, picking up a slip of paper wrapped with the panel. " *'Intent is equal parts courage and imagination,'* "he read. " *'Have the courage to return to the path, follow it to its end, and explore the darkness that lies beneath. When you can recognize that intent will take you where the endless cycle of actions alone cannot, you will find the next verse.'* "

"Go back?" Hannah exclaimed. "We're not going back. You heard Emma, Otto. She said she was going to call the police. It's going to be embarrassing enough having to face her at work."

"We're agreed on this one. I simply do not have the mettle for this." He sighed loudly. "Intent. I don't know about you, but my intent is to remain a free man."

"It's funny what this says about pushing boulders up endless hills. Isn't that a Greek myth? Sisyphus or someone?"

"He's the bloke. Maybe the Greeks and Tibetans passed notes," Otto concluded. "I feel like that here sometimes. Like, why am I working so hard? What am I supposed to be accomplishing? I don't even enjoy myself." He looked around his office.

"Is there something you'd rather be doing?" Hannah asked.

Otto nodded.

"Yeah," she said, "me, too."

Before they locked up to go home, Otto made it a point to take the business card from his desk and placed it carefully in his shirt pocket.

After they parted, Otto thought about what the panel said about courage. He realized that he had been severely lacking it lately in one particular area of his life. Maybe it didn't matter what he did, but he realized that he'd feel a lot better if he could make his intentions known. He made a phone call while walking home that night. His heart was in his throat as he dialed the number.

"Chloe?"

"Aye, Otto." She sounded annoyed.

Otto closed his eyes and just said the words. "I know you're out and about, so I'll keep it short, but there's something I want to say to you." He continued in one breath without pausing, "I love you."

She was silent. Otto heard a voice speaking to Chloe on the other end of the line. It was Ruari.

"What's he saying?" Ruari asked Chloe.

"He says he loves me," Chloe whispered to him. Otto was furious.

"Give me the phone," Ruari said to her. "Otto," Ruari said into the phone. "It's about bloody time, mate!" Ruari said. "Now we just have to figure out a way to trick you into coming home!" Otto's tension broke and he laughed with a lightness he hadn't felt in years.

The next morning Hannah skipped work and went to the hospital to spend the day with her father before his operation. He looked smaller in the hospital bed. Older.

"You scared?" she asked him.

"Me? What do I have to be scared about? Except these young doctors who don't know a damn thing, your mother throwing away my old slippers while I'm gone, and," he paused for a moment, "never waking up to see you, your brother, and your mother again." He gathered himself before his emotions took hold and smiled at Hannah. "But enough about this old man. Did you bring any more of those panels for me to look at?"

Hannah handed her father their latest finds and told him about their misadventure in the garden and getting caught. She left out the part where Otto had kissed her. Her father examined the panels and read the translations. "I know a thing or two about moving boulders uphill with sheer willpower," he said finally. "I worked my ass off to get into medical school. I had to. I wasn't as naturally smart as a lot of my classmates. That didn't matter one bit though. It never occurred to me that being naturally gifted had anything to do with success. I was so determined, studied so hard, that not only did I get in, but I did better than any of them when I got there," he said with some satisfaction.

"Did you ever worry that you were going to fail?" Hannah asked, more for her own benefit than his.

"Worry? Who had time to worry? Thinking about anything but my goal was a luxury your dad didn't have. The people who paused to speculate got shipped home on the next bus out of Chicago. Without that single-minded determination, I wouldn't have made it through. Ninety percent of the battle is just showing up, rain or shine, day after day, with the same strong intention, focused on the result. Once I got that white coat my first day of lab class, I saw myself as a doctor. I was convinced that all I had to do was show up every day and continue to be a doctor. I still have that coat."

"You're forgetting all the work you did. When you were an intern? I think it was a little more than just showing up."

"When you're as focused as I was, you don't notice the work. The only effort I remember was dragging my tired body to the hospital every morning. The rest took care of itself. I don't know how to explain it. When you want it, nothing else matters. The panel's right, all it takes is the imagination to see what you really want, and the courage to show up and get it.

"Don't look at me like you don't know what I'm talking about. I've seen you with that look in your eye, learning how to walk, getting Jake Drummand to take you to the prom. Getting into Berkeley. You've got an iron will, girl. Don't be afraid to use it to get what you want. You started something here. Don't give up until you finish it. Your mother will bail you out if you get arrested."

"Dad!" Hannah exclaimed, horrified.

"You've got only a few panels left to find. I know you

and this Otto person can do it. What's a night in jail compared to learning the secret of enlightenment? Well worth the risk, if you ask me. Don't worry about me, Hannah. No matter what happens, I know I'll be fine. And I'll always be with you."

Before Hannah could respond, her father changed his tone.

"Now go out and get me a pastrami sandwich from the deli across the street. Don't let those nurses see you bring it back in."

Hannah laughed. It was good to have her dad back.

"Mustard?"

"Spicy. And a side of that tapioca pudding they've got. It's not bad."

After the long drive home, Hannah took a hot bath and thought about what her father had said. Then she called Otto.

"Let's do this," she said.

"Awfully big talk for someone who ditched work today, leaving me all alone with the dragon lady. That friend of yours in the bookshop was asking for you. Bob. He's an acrobat?"

"It's a long story," Hannah said. "Are you coming or are you going to make me do this alone?"

"I wouldn't dream of missing this opportunity to get deported. I'll meet you out in front of the library. Just give me a sec to get my trousers on," Otto replied, kicking around the pile on the floor to find his cleanest pair.

"I could have gone my whole life without having to picture that image," Hannah said, crinkling her nose.

"And now, lucky lassie, you won't have to," Otto retorted, pulling his red baseball hat down over his messy curls to guard him against that pair of Fu dogs. He was ready.

Otto had to laugh when he saw Hannah ten minutes later dressed head to toe in black.

"You forgot your ski mask."

"No," Hannah said. "I got it. Just a hat though. I didn't have a mask."

"But you forgot to wear anything red," he said. "The monster dogs are going to realize your intent is all wrong and curse us again."

Hannah shook her head as they set off.

They passed through the Fu dog gate and followed the garden path around the back of the main house. Otto was pleased to see that the waterfall was up and running full force again. He endeavored not to touch anything. The turtle, now residing in the lower koi pond, watched them walk by before plopping off the rock to get a good night's sleep beneath the lily pads.

Hannah and Otto both expected to find some sort of secret passageway, but they were surprised when an old rotten cellar door, built out a few feet from the house, waited for them at the end of the garden path. A small brass plaque on the door read 22b.

"This must have once been a basement apartment or something," Hannah said. She tried the corroded latch. It opened.

Otto put his hand on her shoulder, holding her back for a second.

"We don't need to do this," he said.

"Yes, but we want to," was her reply before she stepped into the cool darkness with her flashlight. Feeling her way down the damp walls, Hannah went step by step into the unknown. Otto followed, closing the door behind them. The stone steps led down farther than they had imagined until they ran out of steps and found themselves on flat ground with a stone wall directly in front of them. Off to the left was a narrow gap in the stone. With nowhere else to go, Hannah and Otto squeezed through.

They found themselves in a narrow corridor that bent slightly to the right. Every few feet were narrow gaps in the wall, identical to the one they had slipped through.

"What is this place?" Hannah whispered as they set out on their way down the corridor.

"Some sort of maze, I guess," Otto said. "Unless we're in catacombs and all these holes in the walls are tombs." They paused to think about that possibility for a moment, their skin crawling.

"Let's just go with the idea it's a maze," Hannah said finally, shaking off the creepy feeling. "What we need to do is check these holes for the panels. I'll check the ones on this side; you check those. You bring a flashlight?"

"No."

"Didn't you even read the clue?" Hannah grumbled. " *'Explore the darkness that lies beneath.'* Doesn't that indicate to you that you might want to bring a flashlight?"

"I brought one last time," he protested. "Hey, I've got a lighter," he said, pulling it out and giving it a quick flick.

He began checking each hole, one after the other, flicking his lighter to illuminate each corridor. Hannah checked her side. There was nothing, and the corridor went on and on. They walked for nearly an hour.

Otto was just about to ask Hannah how big this basement could possibly be when she saw something in the path before them. She bent down to examine the object.

"It's a cigarette. It looks brand-new," she said, picking the object up.

Otto sniffed it. "It smells fresh, right out of the package."

Hannah panicked. "Someone's down here with us. We have to go back."

Otto examined the cigarette more closely and then felt his jacket pocket.

"Uh, Hannah, the cigarette's mine," Otto admitted. "It must have fallen out when I got my lighter out."

"You smoke?" she said, exasperated.

"Only when I'm not drinking," Otto answered.

"That doesn't make sense," she said.

"I know. Most people only smoke when they drink, but . . ." Otto began to explain.

"No, I mean, we found the cigarette in front of us. You dropped it over an hour ago," she said, realizing what that meant. "Otto, we've been walking in circles."

Otto thought about the possibility for a moment. "Not circles. Some other shape. We keep changing directions."

"We're never going to find the panel," Hannah concluded. "Not like this. At this rate, we're never even going to get out of here." Quickly she checked the holes closest to where they had found the cigarette, thinking they might lead back to the stairs. No luck. They all seemed identical inside.

She sat down on the ground and rested her head in her hands. Otto looked around and prayed she wasn't going to cry again.

"Do you care if I smoke?" he asked. Even by the light of her flashlight, he knew she was glaring at him.

"I'm just having a laugh," he said. In some ways, it might be nice to go back to Scotland. At least there people have a sense of humor.

Hannah thought for a few moments and then spoke. "Did you ever hear the story about when Alexander tried to invade Persia?"

"Can't say that I have," Otto said, hoping the story didn't have a grim moral about the dangers of smoking.

"Alexander found himself outnumbered. The king of Persia told him that he could marry his daughter, the princess, and rule the kingdom if Alexander could solve one small puzzle. If he was unable to solve the puzzle, the king would kill him and all of his men."

"Is this about you and me then?" Otto said. "Because I don't think it's going to work out."

"Seriously, Otto. Alexander agreed and the king brought out a big piece of rope tied up in a knot. All Alexander had to do was untangle the knot and the princess and the kingdom would be his. But there was one catch."

"Ah, there always is in stories like this," Otto said. "The princess was a little hard on the eyes?"

"The rope had no ends. It was the endless Gordian knot, like the one on the panel. I think that's what this maze is. An endless knot."

"Why didn't Alexander just cut it? That's what I'd do. Whack. Here's your rope. Give. Me. My. Princess."

Hannah stared at him. "Have you heard this one before? That's exactly what Alexander did."

"So what's your point? Want to knock down these walls? Feeling destructive again? My guess is old lady Wycombe would be down here before you could say 'sand mandala.'"

"No. The clue said that our intent will take us where our actions alone cannot. That's the key to finding this thing," Hannah said.

"It said *above*," Otto corrected. "Our intent would take us *above* our endless actions." They looked at each other for a moment and then Hannah shined her flashlight above their heads and began walking. Less than a few yards away, she saw it. A white endless knot carved in the concrete ceiling, and duct-taped next to it, the next panel.

ILLUMINATING INTENT

What terrifies you? What can stop you in your tracks? Paralyze you in the face of imminent danger? When you were younger, maybe monsters scared you, distant nightmares from a time when beasts on this planet regularly preyed upon us. At night this was the threat that made you yearn for the light, to prove there was nothing to be afraid of.

Now that we are older, the monsters are gone, but the fear remains. It still lurks in darkness, attached to things we can't see. It comes both with the terrible and the glorious. Fears of the unknown, loss, disapproval, humiliation, ridicule, fear of seeming out of control, silence us when we should speak out and keep us from doing what we think is right.

Once fear seeps into our lives, it rots us from the inside. Little by little the power leaks out of our actions until we are tired, depressed, and discouraged. Fear has so many symptoms: It makes us lazy, jealous, and easy to manipulate. But the worst part about fear is the way it uses discouragement, depression, and fatigue to keep us from taking actions to secure our safety. It holds us motionless in terror. How can we guard against fear, or push it out of our lives once it has taken hold and eroded our efficiency? How can we break its paralyzing spell?

We have such a strong reaction to fear because the sensation of fear often precedes the most basic expression of suffering: pain. But after we learn to avoid things that cause us pain, our bodies don't have much use for the fear response.

Earlier in our story, Hannah was reminded that a hot stove might be a potential cause of pain, but the next time she sees a stove, she won't drop her frying pan and run. She will simply be a little more careful.

In fact, there aren't many justifiable causes for alarm in our lives. Sometimes it seems like the fewer actual causes for fear that we live with, the more irrational fears we entertain. When we allow fear to linger where it is not appropriate or rational, it grows and spreads, creating weakness, laziness, and jealousy. Because of its paralyzing nature, when unnecessarily activated, the fear response can pose a threat to our well-being and even, at times, our survival.

Fear is created by the most persistent cause of suffering: ignorance. There is a reason that we are afraid of the dark. Fear and the unknown are inexorably linked. Though our bodies physically respond to fear, fear itself is not an action; it is a feeling generated by our own thoughts. While we can usually accept the physical causality of actions, we can sometimes overlook the importance of our nonphysical influence over them. This influence is *intent*. We can overcome fear only by our own intention to do so.

Sometimes thought of as *will*, intent is inherent in life, the way fibers make up cloth. It is in the weed that sprouts up between a crack in the sidewalk and reaches for the sun. Against all odds and obstacles, life will fight to sustain itself even for an extra second. The body's instinct and compulsion to avoid pain are part of this radical system of self-preservation. On levels as subtle as a pinprick, the body revolts and repulses the threat, so it might continue to perceive, interpret, and respond based on what it has learned.

Intent is a perfect system not unlike physical causality. It has no beginning or end. Even before we developed the complex thoughts and ideas we have now, we were infants with distinct wills to eat, breathe, live, and seek comfort, influenced by our previous learning and environment. Before we were infants we were fetuses in the womb, following urges to move and develop. Even earlier, we were made of two separate cells, from two separate bodies, each pursuing an agenda without even relying on a visible nervous system, two cells that merged to form another unique intent. Whether we believe our intent was gifted to us by a higher will of God, or that it evolved slowly, as long as life continues somewhere in the vast realm of existence, we cannot trace its beginnings or end. Its power to shape the world is undeniable.

This firsthand knowledge of the world through perception, interpretation, and interaction is the method by which we overcome many forms of ignorance. This quest for understanding is natural. Every day we live, we learn more about the world, how things work, how people relate to each other. We try to make our world a little bit closer to the way we'd like it to be, trying to be a little happier. We don't think of this as battling ignorance because it seems so common and mundane. We see our lives through daily dramas, small ups and downs. We see our relationships to others, the boredom and the excitement. But when we step back and look at a human life, it is clear: We are born with little information, skills, or defenses. As we grow, we perceive, interpret, and interact; we learn. We share what we know with others.

When we look at the scope of humanity, even over the past few hundred years, we see that we keep adding to our store of knowledge. We continue to expand the depth of our awareness of others, the world, and ourselves. From the depths of the oceans to the surface of Mars, the average human today understands so much more than the average human of even a hundred years ago. Enlightenment is freedom from ignorance and suffering. Even without doing anything special, humanity inches a little bit closer to that liberation every day, and we do this naturally using our intent.

Our human intent is a mix of the imagination to envision new possibilities and the courage to make those possibilities a reality. This combination drives us into the world, guides our attention, and shapes our actions, thus shaping the world. Intent is the strongest power tool in the universe, but so often we use it thoughtlessly, never imagining the incredible potential available to us when we harness our imagination and courage.

To create any possibility, begin by simply imagining the world as different from what it is. Different how? In any way imaginable. So often we limit ourselves by simply not thinking big enough. We should let our imaginations run wild and exercise our creativity. Someone once said, Whatever you can conceive, you can achieve—and that person was right. All we need is the courage to back up our imagination.

Courage is the quality of being that enables one to face danger and fear with self-possession, confidence, resolution, and bravery. It shares the determination of effort, but it is so much more. It is a force inherent in all life. And it has to be. We already know that life is full of struggles. Our only reward is either fleeting bodily pleasure, or the opportunity to minimize suffering long enough to understand how the system of existence works, in other words, enlightenment. To get through all that we must be determined. There are plenty of obstacles in the way, and we will create many more for ourselves, but we possessed the will to continue to struggle even before we knew our goal.

Hannah's father is beginning to understand this will to persist. Even after a life of apathy about his health, faced with his own mortality, he is suddenly willing to take measures he never considered in order to continue to live.

But how often do we exercise our courage? How often do we imagine life in a whole new way and then act to bring that potential to life? More often than we might imagine. Most everything we do is an exercise of intent. At lunchtime we imagine what we'd like out of the choices available and then we have the courage to open the fridge or order something off the menu. When Hannah got ready to meet Otto, she imagined the perfect outfit to conceal her on her mission, and she had the courage to take it out of her closet and put it on. When Otto thought his relationship with Chloe was endangered, he imagined the solution of expressing his true feelings to her and then had the courage to call her up. Otto and Hannah have imagined the possibilities of following Drake's clues to discover the backdoor to enlightenment, and then had the courage to pursue their goal all the way into their boss's cellar. We are all experts at subconsciously exercising our intent, so why not consciously use this powerful tool to build the lives we really want?

When we think of human greatness, we look to people who, through their imagination and courage, have furthered our understanding of the way the world and our own consciousness work. We admire people who by the expert use of their intent reveal to us the outer limits of skill, talent, character, and influence. These are the things we value most, and the people who show us these possibilities are our heroes. Humanity is ever reaching toward the understanding and lack of suffering that enlightenment represents. Our only complaints can be that our heroes are too few and we lack the imagination and courage to follow them.

Why are we lacking in heroes? If courage is such a vital factor in our will to live, then why do most people shirk it? Why do we kneel when we might stand, as though we're terrified to display even the tiniest light, out of fear that giant moths will come and smother it? But it is not giant moths or any other supernatural monster that we fear. We are afraid of each other.

When we don't speak in front of a crowd, it isn't that we're afraid the crowd will lynch us because of our ideas; we are afraid we will look foolish and they will laugh at us. When we write what is popular rather than what is true, we don't do so because we are still afraid that we will be burned on a pile of our own books for heresy; we are only afraid that not enough people will read our words. When we are afraid to take a stand against injustice, it isn't because we are afraid we will die on the gallows charged with sedition; we don't take a stand because we are afraid we will lose our jobs, our endorsements, and our popularity. We do what we are praised for doing, what we are paid to do, and these golden handcuffs have proven more effective in stifling our voices than the centuries of torture and murder that free thinkers have faced in the past.

We want to look, act, and think like everyone else. That's why popular things are prized far beyond any intrinsic value they might have. We know that we fear what is different in other men, and we do not want to arouse each other's suspicions. But we are no strangers to courage. We knew this quality intimately before we exiled it from our lives rather than have others discover it within us and despise us for it.

Not only do we fail ourselves, but also far from inspiring one another to greatness or heroics we discourage each other from doing the things we cannot do—or refuse to do—ourselves. For every nine people who denounce innovation, only one will encourage it. For every nine people who want what the world can offer them, only one will want only what he can offer himself. For every nine people who do things the way they have always been done, only one will ever wonder if there is a better way. For every nine people who stand in line in front of a locked building, only one will ever come around and check the backdoor.

Our progress as a species rests squarely on the shoulders of that tenth person. The nine are satisfied with things they are told are valuable. Person 10 determines for himself what has value. The nine look around for inspiration. Person 10 looks forward. The nine do what they are told. Person 10 does what he knows is right. The nine aim for safety. Person 10 aims for enlightenment. Be Person 10.

We all must lead ourselves to goals and potentials that are ours alone. To attain enlightenment we must each be what only we can be and do what no other can do.

When we understand this, we realize how insane it is to discourage imagination and diversity. If we are to be all that we can be, we must give each other the space we need to dream and reach our acme. If we are to enjoy the benefits of all humanity can offer, we must be able to see we are each anomalies. Embracing this fact helps us along the path of greatness; if we choose to deny it, we take the path of sheep. The choice is ours.

We can use our intent to attain great material wealth, fame, romance, or to feed the hungry and house the poor. We now recognize the impermanence of the world, and we are free to behave in any way we choose. We realize the effects of our actions and the influence of our thoughts. With a little contemplation and effort we can go after the goals that interest us. But after we attain those goals, then what?

Though we will have improved our condition a great deal and maybe even eliminated much suffering, we will still suffer in different ways. We can labor an entire lifetime for the material benefit of others, and we will not eliminate the suffering in the world. We can feed the entire world, and in a few hours they will be hungry again. We can provide great wealth to every impoverished person in the world and still all people will suffer for different reasons. That is the nature of impermanence. The work would certainly keep us very busy, but is that the best we can expect from our lives? Busywork to fulfill the whims of others?

In a world of impermanence, there is no coming or going that makes any difference whatsoever. Like Otto and Hannah wandering through their maze, actions only perpetuate an endless cycle of more actions. We cannot escape this cycle physically. To achieve our goals, we must also engage our minds. By reducing our ignorance, we will suffer less.

The first three perfections were about our relation to the outside world, about the impermanence of our form, the freedom of our attitudes, and the causal nature of our actions. The sufferings they dealt with are struggles that also come from interaction with the outside world: pain and discontent, constructs, and pervasive action are all fueled by action and our interpretations of what we perceive.

These last three perfections—intent, being, and unity—require no senses, no movement, and no interaction, only consciousness. They can be realized alone in a room. The suffering they deal with arises only from us. To truly help others and ourselves we must use understanding to continue to dissolve the final and most fundamental cause of suffering: ignorance.

Realizing the perfection of courage is understanding that all actions are empty without intent. When we understand the truth in this, and appropriately seek an enlightened life like a man dying of thirst, we will realize enlightenment in an instant.

THE BACKDOOR APPROACH: INTENT

Physical actions aren't the only things that have an effect on the kind of life you will lead. Your thoughts also influence not only your experience but also whether or not your desires will manifest into realities. Your own intent determines what course your life will take. Even if you take the physical actions necessary to realize your goals, unless you back those actions up with supporting thoughts and strong intentions, you could be wasting your efforts.

The next step of the backdoor approach is devising a strategy of thoughts you will employ to bring your goal to fruition. By now you all know the power of positive thinking, but you also really need to focus your intentions to accomplish your aims. This is simply a matter of keeping your eyes on the prize. Be aware of negative thoughts and mental constructs that can sneak back in and distract you.

Sometimes you fail to achieve your dreams because you forget what they are before they even get the chance to come true! You can get sidetracked and give your valuable attention to any passing whim, when you should guard your intent very carefully. Your intent is your most indispensable asset to achieve your aspirations.

Step Five: FOCUS your intentions and hold them steady.

Allow time for the effects of your actions to unfold. This is a delicate time when it can be easy to get discouraged. Impatience can be another pitfall. Don't sabotage the measures you took by engaging with conflicting thoughts and actions. If you're in a hurry to experience feelings of accomplishment, it can be tempting to abandon your real desires and pursue something you imagine is easier to attain. In reality, all you're doing is wasting energy. Stick with your goals and you will see them through to fruition.

To aid in this task, summarize each goal in a brief verbal intention. Word these declarations very specifically. Avoid being vague. Design the statement to reflect your goal as if it were an ongoing process, not in the future or past tense. You don't want to convince yourself that your goal is forever out of reach or has already happened and you missed it! Write it down; repeat it regularly. For example:

> *I love my new, reliable (type of car).*
> *I have a loving relationship with (name).*
> *I make ($?) a year as a(n) (occupation).*
> *I am an enlightened being.*

Repeat this intention each morning when you get up to help guide your day in the direction of your dreams. Repeat it throughout the day to ward off distractions. Say it to yourself each night before you go to bed to subconsciously program yourself to stay on track.

Give yourself nonverbal cues as well. Involve all your senses. Cut out pictures that represent your dreams and pin them up where you'll notice them throughout the day. Snap a picture of your dream house to keep on the screen of your cell phone. Put a CD in your car that will remind you of your new romantic relationship each time you turn on your car stereo. Use coconut-scented lotion to keep you focused on the vacation you're saving up for. The important thing is to fully engage your mind with your ambition. **Visualize:** Close your eyes. Breathe fully and deeply, allowing yourself to completely relax. Imagine yourself smiling as you climb in a gorgeous mountain range, filled with beautiful trees and huge boulders. Smell the fresh plants and rich earth as you enjoy the scenic view of the valley below. Feel the crisp mountain air on your face. You spot a peak nearby that towers into the clouds with a large rocky face at its summit. Feeling strong and energetic, you gather the courage to climb this peak. Overcoming obstacle after obstacle, you make your way to the top, never losing heart or momentum. When you reach the pinnacle, you notice a hammer and chisel resting on the blank slate of rock at your feet. Recall your intention. Take the hammer and chisel in your hands and carve your intention deeply into the stone. Brush aside the dust and read it to yourself in the sun with a feeling of accomplishment. It will remain there unchanged forever.

BENEFITS

Intent is the bridge between laziness and action, between despair and industry. Without the excuses and entitlements you have created for yourself, you have only the courage of life to press on even in the most trying and desperate situations.

Knowing what you know now, the next time you feel

lazy, look for constructs blocking your natural impulse to grow. Evaluate your plans; remove the beliefs and constructs that would hinder you and then act. Stick with your objectives and do not use your indecision as an excuse to procrastinate. This is how you avoid getting in a rut. Never fear action as much as stagnation.

When you allow yourself to be manipulated, you are just being lazy. You erroneously think it is easier to let others make decisions for you than to make the decisions yourself. Cowards do not escape the law of causality. Just because you follow someone else's orders doesn't mean that you can escape blame. Orders are influence; action is cause. It's more satisfying to suffer for the results of your own ideas than someone else's.

When you feel jealous, stop looking around! If you were more concerned with what your own goals are and less concerned with distractions, you wouldn't have this problem. People can hardly live their own lives and yet they insist on concerning themselves with the lives of others. Instead of wasting your time with jealousy, notice courage in the people you admire. Would they have gotten as far as they have if they had wasted all their efforts watching you? Now go do what needs to be done.

If you dislike your job, alter the situation—the job, your attitude—to make the circumstances more pleasant. There is no virtue in begrudgingly doing anything. If you can't figure out how to be satisfied where you are, then change your location. The goal of life is to strive, learn, and grow. Even the most basic organisms have this right. You at least deserve the same quality of life as a fungus, bacteria, or protozoa. The next time you are at your desk ask yourself, Would even a fungus be happy here under these conditions? If you honestly answer no, then maybe you should move on.

You have the power to accomplish everything you want to do. Use courage and imagination to achieve your goals and reduce ignorance. Realizing the perfection of intent fosters enthusiasm and self-esteem, removing laziness, envy, and discouragement. With a sharply focused intent, nothing can stop you.

THE ESSENCE OF INTENT

*"A seeker who does not rely on actions to practice
virtuous effort knows there is no point pushing a
boulder up an endless hill; he will never reach the
end of his endeavor. The boulder can easily be
moved in his mind."*

- **The Perfection of Intent** is a mix of the imagination to envision new possibilities and the courage to make those possibilities a reality. It guides our attention, shapes our actions, thus shaping the world.
- **The Backdoor Approach**
  Step Five: FOCUS your intentions and hold them steady.
- **Exercise**   Sum up your goal in a brief verbal intention. Repeat it each morning and night.
- **Benefits**   Recognizing the perfection of intent also helps with symptoms of ignorance such as
  - depression
  - discouragement
  - laziness
  - being easily manipulated
  - jealousy
- **Conclusion**   Recognize that intent can take you where the endless cycle of action cannot.

If you cannot be a poet, be the poem.

—DAVID CARRADINE

6 | The perfection of Being

"You're just going to have to stand up then," Otto whispered in the cellar maze. "I'll steady you."

Somewhere above him Hannah balanced on his shoulders, unable to reach the package taped to the concrete ceiling, but unwilling to boost herself up any higher than her knees. Otto wobbled beneath her weight.

"This coming from the man who told me he'd catch me if I jumped out of a tree—and then didn't. No way."

"I'd be happy to switch places," Otto whispered angrily. "It'd be a lot easier than trying to support you. You have absolutely no balance whatsoever. Like a sack of potatoes."

"Hold on," Hannah said. She struggled to her feet, using his head as a support. Otto teetered, and in the second before she lost her balance completely she launched herself at the package, catching the edge of it tightly in her hand. It came off the ceiling with a rip. She hit the stone floor on both hands and one knee.

Otto began unwrapping the package as soon as it hit the ground.

"You're welcome," Hannah said. "And don't worry about me. I'm fine."

"Expertly done. Maybe you can join your friend Bob-the-acrobat in a two-man show."

By the light of Hannah's flashlight, the black panel nearly disappeared in the darkness, making the golden vase drawn at its center appear to float in the air before them. After examining it for a moment, Otto shuffled through the panel's wrapping for the translation. He found it. They both read in silence.

"A seeker who relies on thoughts to practice concentration is like a person trying to pour nectar in a vase filled with sand. Only when he removes the sand will he find room for the nectar. Be still and just exist. To realize enlightenment, one must recognize the simple perfection of being."

Otto flipped through the pages of the wrapper slowly at first and then frantically. "There's no clue here," he said. "Just this translation."

"That's impossible. Give me that," Hannah said.

"Suit yourself," Otto said, handing her the pile of paper. "I tell you, it's not there."

"Well, it has to be, because there is no other way out of here," Hannah insisted.

Hannah noticed his accent became much thicker when he was upset. She, too, searched through the papers, front and back, and examined the panel again, while Otto fumbled around flicking his lighter, searching for a way out.

Finally they gave up. They each reached the conclusion the other had already guessed: Drake had not left them a clue this time, and whatever passage had once opened to let them in was now lost to them.

Hannah turned off the flashlight to save the batteries. She felt like crying and Otto wanted to punch something. With only rock surrounding him, he decided to temporarily curb his impulse.

"Okay, let's think this through," Otto started. He slid down the wall to settle uncomfortably on the hard floor. He could feel the chill of the stone through his trousers. "Do you have your cell phone?" he finally asked.

"Who are we going to call? We're going to get arrested," Hannah whimpered.

"You have it. Good. Do you have reception down here?"

Hannah checked. Zero bars.

"Should we scream for help?" Hannah asked. "The

Wycombes are home now. But in the morning . . ." she trailed off. "They'll be gone all day. No one will hear us."

"Think about it, Hannah. Have you heard anything from our neighbors above? A TV set? A voice? Because I haven't. We've just got to sit tight and think this one through."

His words made her heart sink as reality set in. They might not get arrested, but they might not ever be found. They discussed their options and possibilities for a long time. Hannah insisted they figure out a method to systematically check all the gaps in the wall for the exit, and Otto thought the key was to figure out the mechanism that closed the door, and how it could be reopened.

Eventually their conversation dwindled and they fell silent. At least for the moment they gave up. Otto rested with his feet up on the wall, and Hannah curled up, glad that for once she had brought a sweater. Not long after they made themselves as comfortable as they could under the circumstances, a heavy click sounded and one by one overhead fluorescent lights switched on down the hall, illuminating the entire space.

They both sat up and waited patiently to be discovered, but no one came. Puzzled, they wandered around the maze, seeing it for the first time in the light. It was a lot smaller than they had imagined, and shaped like interlocking figure eights.

"Here's our exit," Hannah called out from a gap in the wall. "I don't know how we missed it."

"We didn't miss anything," Otto said. "It must have re-opened when the lights came up."

"When we stopped talking," Hannah added.

"And moving," Otto said. "These lights must have been on a sound and motion detector. I guess whoever hid these panels really valued peace and quiet."

"Or really wanted to teach us a lesson. They must have had the timer set for the lights to go on after ten minutes. It felt like an eternity."

"That was nothing. All we had to do was sit down and shut up for ten minutes. Did you know that some people are so good at meditating that they can sit perfectly still and hold one image steady in their minds for, like, four hours?"

"And what's the point of that?" Hannah asked.

"I don't know. I bet they're really mellow people though."

Hannah shook her head. "Or boring. Let's get out of here."

But Otto was distracted. He pointed to a place where the ceiling was low. That panel in the concrete ceiling appeared different from the others around it. Otto reached up and knocked on it. *Tattarrattat*. It was wood finished to look like concrete. A closer inspection revealed a small groove in the panel. Otto slipped his thumb in and pressed down. The panel swung down. Attached to it was the bottom step in a wide ladder that led up to another trapdoor. Otto climbed up the ladder, pushed the door up, and peeked out. He was shocked to find himself looking straight across the entryway of Drake's old house. Across the sea of mahogany flooring, he saw a massive grandfather clock staring back at him. The big number 12 at the top dominated its face.

Hannah climbed up next to Otto and peered out. As she watched the seconds tick by, she thought of her father. He might be nearly out of time. She thought about the time they had spent together when she was a little girl. He had taken the family for a train ride to the Grand Canyon in the snow. She could still see the smoke billowing out from the train as her father tossed her a sandwich. He was always trying to feed her. "If you put it in front of her," he'd always said to her mother, "she'll eat it." Hannah smiled sadly.

She could only recall memories now; she couldn't imagine something she and her dad would do together in the future, what it would be like when he woke up. It must be like that when people die, Hannah thought. In your mind, they get stuck forever in the past tense.

Watching the time pass made Otto think of different things. Sometime in the near future his little boy soon would come into the world free—for a few years anyway—of time. With no past, life would seem to stretch out infinitely before him. Otto tried to remember what it was like, having a whole life ahead of him, feeling immortal, blissfully ignorant of how years are capable of flying by. He thought about his boy growing up, watching him grow old. He imagined Chloe there with him.

Suddenly they heard a noise and were jolted out of their time travels. They quickly lowered the door and backed down the ladder.

"Did you hear something?" Otto said.

"Maybe. I don't know. I think I just got spooked."

"Want to see something else spooky?"

"Not particularly," Hannah said. Otto pointed to the riser of the top stair anyway. Written there was the question *"Can you stop the hands of time?"*

"The ladder must be psychic," Otto said, "because I was just thinking that."

"Me, too." There was a creaking from above. "Okay, that time I definitely heard something," Hannah said. Otto went up the ladder and raised the trapdoor ever so slightly.

In a room off the entryway a television set was on with the volume turned completely down. A soccer game. Otto could see the back of a man's head over the back of an armchair. It must be Mr. Wycombe, he thought. Otto watched the player Ronaldo pass the ball to Rooney, who took a shot. He missed. At the same time, Otto and Mr. Wycombe shook their heads in disgust. When Emma came into the room, instantly the TV switched off and Otto disappeared back beneath the floor.

"What's going on up there?" Hannah asked.

"Man U is playing Chelsea," Otto explained. "Rooney missed a shot."

"Is anyone out there?" Hannah asked.

"Yeah. The old dragon busted him watching soccer. I think she's making him go up to bed. My mom used to do it to my dad all the time," Otto said.

"I think I know what to do," said Hannah. "Did you see that gold vase on top of the clock? You need to go up there and stop the clock. What else could that mean?"

"Then what?" Otto asked.

"Then we'll see what happens."

"Oh, that's a fine plan you've got!" Otto exclaimed.

"Better than yours," Hannah countered.

"Which is?" Otto asked.

"Watch soccer through the floor until we get caught," Hannah whispered. "Don't you have cable?"

Otto shrugged. He really would have liked to see Rooney make that goal.

They waited until they were certain that the Wycombes had gone upstairs to bed before Otto crept out, slowly opened the glass door of the clock, and reached in to stop the pendulum.

"Wait!" Hannah whispered.

Just then, on the quarter hour, the clock rang out Westminster chimes. Shocked, Otto jumped back, letting the door of the clock case fall closed with a bang.

"What was that?" they heard Emma say from upstairs.

Hannah glared at Otto to hurry. He reached back in and stopped the pendulum. From where she was hiding, Hannah could see the package drop down from the clock-works, but from Otto's perspective, nothing had happened. Hannah took a deep breath, sprang out of the hatch, grabbed the package, and went back for the trap-door, which was so well disguised in the glossy floor planks that Hannah didn't even know where to look for it. Otto grabbed her arm and pulled her into a room off the foyer. He closed the door behind them just as Emma came down the stairs.

In the living room, Emma saw a small gray animal crouched near the fireplace. A raccoon. Taking an umbrella from the rack by the door, she sprung to turn on the lights. In the light, Emma found that the animal was only a throw blanket that had slipped off the arm of the sofa. She replaced the umbrella. Before she returned upstairs, however, she was surprised to find that the enormous clock in her entryway had inexplicably, suddenly stopped.

ILLUMINATING BEING

What are you doing right now? You weren't reading. You are reading now, but you weren't at that moment. Try it again. What are you doing now? By the time you finished that sentence, you had stopped reading and were busy thinking about the question. Maybe you were tapping your foot; maybe you were looking up at the ceiling. Breathing. Digesting. Wondering what the noise is in the next room. Thinking about something that happened earlier? Wondering what is coming next? Wondering where we are going with this line of thought? What are you doing now? What about now?

If we become aware of our thoughts, we'll notice that they really don't have much to do with what is going on in front of us or in our bodies. Our thoughts are all over the place. How can we keep track of anything with a mind this squirrelly, never mind realize enlightenment?

The remedy for this problem is concentration, or meditation. In the most basic sense, there are two types of meditation. The first kind is *analytical meditation*. This is focusing our thoughts and attention on a phenomenon or problem to understand how it works. We don't need to sit on pillows in a monastery to do this kind of meditation. Whether the obstacle is how to overcome the world's suffering or how to work a new computer, analytical meditation is one way we can understand our everyday world.

Hannah and Otto demonstrated this kind of meditation when they attempted to figure out how to get out of the labyrinth. Through focusing on the problem at hand, exploring its components and possible solutions, without even realizing it, our heroes engaged in meditation.

The second kind of meditation is *stabilizing meditation*. When people think about meditation, this is what they imagine. In stabilizing meditation, the goal is to sit still for an extended time and empty the mind or direct the attention on a single object like breath, thought, or an image.

With practice, over time, it is possible to sit for longer periods of time and focus on the object of contemplation without great effort, or without becoming either too sleepy or too excited. And just as Otto described, many people can mentally see the object in clear detail. When a person can sit without distraction from body, mind, or the outside world for four hours, he or she is said to have achieved something called *calm abiding*. These individuals will see the world more clearly, like a placid sea more accurately reflects the sky than a tempestuous one.

Many people get a lot of enjoyment from both kinds of meditation, and the benefits are undeniable, unless you feel like denying them. There are times in life when a rest from the barrage of your thoughts is necessary and healthy. Meditation can aid in relaxation and gaining composure to view the world calmly.

But will watching our breath for hours or days necessarily help us realize enlightenment? It is certainly an impressive skill, like tightrope walking or acrobatics, and requires no less concentration. But it is only a skill. Enlightenment is not a triple axel with a ten-point landing or a wheelie. It isn't a trick; it is an understanding, like knowing the earth is round and revolves around the sun. Concentration is critical for any realization—to from remembering where we left our glasses all the way to realizing enlightenment. Without the ability to fix our mind on an object, we would be lost both in the world and in our thoughts. Being is not a construct. It is the continuity of our existence. But the idea that we must sit, focused on an arbitrary object for hours at a time in order to realize enlightenment is a construct. It is only a belief. If you like to sit for hours, it can be your belief. If you don't, then let it go.

What is being? To be is to exist, to have a reality. Being is not a mental construct; it is the most fundamental state attainable. It doesn't even require life. The perfection of being is not the addition of anything extra to this state, but rather realizing this state as purely as possible. And to do that, you must remove from being one construct that we invariably affix to it, our concept of time. After we realize the perfection of intent and proceed beyond fear to uncover the root of ignorance, we must thoroughly proceed beyond the rest of our constructs, too. For the most part, our most basic constructs add another dimension to our awareness, but they don't really compromise our ability to function in the world. The amazing construct of language is an example of this. We don't need the word *green* to see the color green, nor does the existence of the word itself limit the way we see the color.

But not all basic constructs are so benign. Once we move beyond fear and realize we have the courage to see the world as it is, we must finally confront our notions about a basic aspect of reality: time. While our concept of time is supremely useful in communication, organization, and survival, our mistaken beliefs about time directly impede our realization of enlightenment. Our ideas about time undercut our happiness and contribute to ignorance in ways so insidious and pervading, the suffering they produce is hardly recognized. But to realize enlightenment, we don't need to escape time and live at the center of a black hole; we just need to see beyond the illusion that our ideas about time create.

To overcome ignorance, having the courage to seek wisdom isn't enough; you also must have the time. Luckily, we have all the time in the world. We have the endless present moment. The perfection of being is that we exist in the present moment every moment.

This basic realization, that you exist in the present moment, is difficult to comprehend. Being is so fundamental that it is easy to take it for granted, like the virtuous effort of your beating heart. Through the course of our lives, we probably will not spend more than a few minutes thinking about our heart beating. But we will become instantly convinced of the importance of our beating heart when it stops.

Our consciousness is tied to the present moment.

Our awareness can't outrun time, and it can't anchor itself and stay behind while time goes on ahead without it.
We march on with time, hand in hand. But it doesn't
seem that way, does it? Time seems to slip from the future
right into the past, barely even grazing the present as it
zips by. We always spend so long looking forward to
something, but once it arrives, it passes by quickly, and
then we spend ages remembering it. Our consciousness
seems to spend more time in the past and the future than
in the present. How is this possible?

Unless we can find some sort of time machine that no
one has yet discovered, we cannot get to the past, future,
or any tense but the present. And yet we allow our minds
to wander into delusions—fictitious pasts and futures—
that do not exist. The past does not exist as we remember
it; we only retain the interpretation of our perception. As
time goes by, we often add a good dose of wishful thinking or storytelling, until we transform that interpretation
into complete fiction.

Hannah's memories of her father may or may not be
accurate. She can filter them to remember the good
things when she has tender feelings and the bad things
when she feels angry. On top of cherry-picking her memories for content, her emotions color them. Otto also
fabricates his ideas about the future. Would Chloe have
made the cut in his fantasy last week when he was irritated with her? It doesn't matter. He has no way of know-

ing what the future holds. The future does not exist as any of us imagine it; our imaginings are only projections, again, fiction.

We enjoy thinking about the past and future so much that we can give these thoughts much of our attention— a lot more than they deserve considering that they are nothing more than fantasies. We spend time remembering something that is colored by thoughts, or projecting a future that is the complete fabrication of our mind, when all the while we rob ourselves of the only time that does exist, the present.

Oddly enough, our perception/interpretation response is tethered slightly behind the present moment. By the time we realize that we have seen a bear, the bear has already moved. The action that caused the thunder we hear happened seconds ago. It takes time for information to reach us, and then for us to interpret the data. We only sense things after they happen, and then after we understand them. Our minds can be quick to interpret stimuli but can never interpret them simultaneously as they occur.

Our perceptions only deliver information about what is now old news. Sitting in a field and listening to birds chirping, we hear only echoes from the past of other nearby locations. We are always a step behind. If we want to respond to the world with any degree of efficiency, we must do more than simply react to what we perceive; we must grasp the trend of the stimuli and anticipate the path it will take in the immediate future.

Take the soccer game that Otto watched from the door in the floor. When Ronaldo passed the ball to his running teammate, he aimed it where he thought Rooney would be by the time Rooney had traveled the distance ahead toward the goal. Ronaldo had to kick the ball forcefully enough to move it beyond the place Rooney was, to where Rooney would be. If he aimed the ball to where Rooney was when he kicked it, he would never complete the pass; his teammate would be long gone.

The same goes for driving. When Hannah drives to visit her parents, she takes the freeway. When she decides to change lanes, she has to take into consideration that she and the other cars are moving at different speeds. She has to anticipate where the cars around her will be at the time she switches lanes. If she simply reacts, she will always be too late.

Usually when we interpret our senses, we rely on information from the past to predict the future. Well, what about the present? We perceive things, but we cannot know the state or location of the sources of those stimuli at the present moment from the information we have gathered. The air around us might smell like apple pie, but that doesn't mean that there is an apple pie nearby. We can perceive that light is hitting our eyes, but by the time we register that, it is possible that the source has moved elsewhere. We can feel that a sound wave has hit our eardrum, but we cannot know anything about the source or location of that sound in that instant.

Our senses can tell us about our present state in our immediate location, but not the present state of the stimuli in their locations. This means that if we really want to fully experience the present moment, even for an instant, we must recognize the input from our senses as echoes from the past. We don't have to shut our senses off or ignore them. We don't have to stop doing or stop reacting. Remember, there is no point in trying to stop or slow down life. But when we realize the perfection of being, we can't be deceived by our senses and imagine they can give us current information about anything except what is going on right now in our eyes, ears, nose, mouth, and skin.

Most of the time we don't perceive things accurately anyway. Look around in the room you are in. Do you really see it as it is? Do you see the wear in the items there? The dust that might have collected on them? We tend to memorize things, and often we see what we expect to see instead of what is there. When you see a family photograph, do you see paper and colored ink or do you see an image of a loved one? The special meaning we attach to objects veils our perception. Look at that picture again. Look at the shape of the body or bodies in it. Is that shape consistent with how you would perceive the people if they stood before you? Our brains regularly fill in missing or distorted details in our perception to form recognizable images. If you watch an old 8mm film, you will focus on creating a continuous image in your mind rather than focusing on the jumps and flecks that distract from the image. After a while you might not even notice the imperfections and will see only the meaning, but what has changed, the quality of the tape or your mind?

Our eyes and ears are the biggest offenders because we use them to interpret language and visual cues that might have constructed meaning assigned to them. We are accustomed to filling in the blanks or construing meaning from approximations. Think of handwriting. Everyone has different handwriting, but unless it is terrible or the language is one you can't read, you will most likely be able to decipher it. When we listen to each other speak the same language, we allow for a broad range of accents before we are unable to interpret meaning from speech.

Emma experienced this when she mistook a blanket for a raccoon. When Otto carelessly slammed the clock case shut, Emma thought a raccoon in the kitchen seemed the most likely explanation for the racket. She was so impressed with her idea that she looked for evidence to back it up. When none was available, her mind created support for her raccoon theory out of the shadows cast by a throw blanket. Lucky for the blanket, Emma investigated further before she charged at it.

Our senses such as taste and touch are more literal. We rely on these two senses to keep us from danger, and we don't mess around too much with interpretation. When we feel pain, we react or move immediately. We don't wait around trying to establish what it might mean or decide if it poses a real threat or not. The same goes for taste. If something tastes terrible, we spit it out, trusting that our bodies have developed this response to substances that are dangerous to our health. We can unlearn this response, of course. A child's taste response to an alcoholic drink will usually be more violent than an adult's response. And then, through our constructs, we learn to dull our senses further.

A great deal of ignorance arises from our frustration with our inability to capture the present moment. We are accustomed to using the extensive network of the nervous system to reach out to the world, but no matter how hard we try, it is not possible to use our nervous system to gain current information about the state of anything but itself. Further, if we cannot grasp the present moment—the time in which we exist—how can we be certain that we do exist at all? In our frustration, we become obsessed with the past and the future. We try to create our own reality where we have all the time in the world to prove our own existence and draw conclusions

about anything and everything, in other words, to be omniscient. But our minds cannot undo what has been done,
or control every element in an event that will happen in
the future. Our creations are nothing more than a delusion.

But attempting to locate and cling to the present tense
is like trying to find your eyeglasses when they are on
your face. No matter what we think about—past, present, or future—and no matter if we follow our senses'
cues to our bodies or ignore them and sit in meditation,
we are living in the present tense. This isn't because we
are especially skilled or lucky; it is because the present
tense is the only one available to things that exist. Abandoning this struggle and realizing that we exist in the
present moment is the next step to overcoming the obstacle of ignorance.

THE BACKDOOR APPROACH: BEING

It is so easy to get caught up in the pervasive action of
everyday life. Sometimes no matter how much you focus
your intent, life can feel like swimming in a stormy sea.
With waves hitting you from every angle, it's hard enough
just to keep your head above water, never mind attempt
to swim for a destination.

Here's where you can use the perfection of being like
a magical remote control to put everything in slow mo-

tion until you can figure out how to respond to your environment.

Step Six: ALLOW yourself to be in the present moment.

Build time into every day, either when you get up in the morning, when you go to sleep at night—or, for the best results, both—to perform the following exercise. You can use this exercise to replace simply verbalizing your intention as discussed in the previous chapter.

Visualize: Choose a place to perform this exercise where it is quiet and calm. Place a pen and notepad nearby. Use earplugs and a soft, dark mask if necessary to block out any distractions. Make yourself comfortable and close your eyes.

Use your intention like a mantra, repeating it repeatedly in your mind, synching it with slow inhalations and exhalations. Other thoughts of the past and future will pop into your mind, but simply watch them arise and dissipate as you repeat your intention. Before too long, your mind will settle into the rhythm of your repeated intention. You'll know that you are experiencing the present moment when you feel calm, focused, and at ease.

Now analyze your intention. See the circumstances surrounding it clearly in your mind. Step-by-step, work out how your goal will unfold. If you feel overwhelmed or are currently facing a challenge, analyze the problem further in this relaxed state. The situation will become clearer and clearer to you, and angles you had not previously considered will be revealed. When you have a strong picture of how your goal will unfold, how your challenges can be surmounted, and how you will respond to your situation, repeat your intention again a few times. Open your eyes and write down the insights you have discovered.

If during the course of the day you feel overwhelmed, distracted, scattered, or you're simply not being as efficient as you could be, take five. Shut your door, go to the restroom, or even go sit in your car, and perform this exercise. Once you get in synch with the rhythm of your surroundings, the sea that once appeared rough transforms into predictable peaks and valleys.

This exercise trains your mind to respond to thinking about your goal with clarity, relaxation, and efficiency. When you say your intention to yourself, you will indicate to your mind that you are now ready to peacefully and efficiently get down to business and produce results. Soon, simply repeating your intention, in any situation, will produce feelings of calm, clarity, and control. No matter what kind of challenges you face, take advantage of this method to give you a boost throughout your day, while subconsciously reinforcing your goal.

BENEFITS

When you realize the perfection of being, you will see that guilt and regret are symptoms of living in the past. When you are unable to anticipate and respond to stimuli in time to gain a favorable result, you can feel frustrated. This might lead you to attempt to relive the situation repeatedly in your mind until you create the perfect fantasy result. Understand that the time for that particular action has come and gone. If you want to have any chance at all of avoiding regret in the future, instead of spending all your time fantasizing about what you might have done, start paying attention to the situation at hand. You might not be able to respond exactly to the present moment, but you'll be most effective if you respond as quickly as possible to the newest information available. Being obsessed with a dreamworld will not help you to be more aware of current events and stimuli.

Do you take unnecessary risks? Are you a thrill seeker? Thrill seeking is just an extreme way to draw your attention to the present moment. When you are in danger or your life is at risk, all else seems to disappear and there is only the present moment and the task at hand. Once you realize the perfection of being, this feeling exists whether you are mowing the lawn, sitting at your desk, or skydiving.

Not finishing what you start, indecision, and attention

disorders stem from attempts to live in the future. No matter what you are doing, you imagine that there is something better, something more rewarding, just around the corner, and you don't want to miss a thing. You dart from this thing to that, hoping to get to sample it all. It's like the behavior of a man who buys a ticket to a multiplex movie theater and spends his two hours sneaking into every movie that's playing. As soon as he settles into one movie, he wonders what he is missing in the next theater, so he runs over and checks. At the end of his two hours, he has seen bits and pieces of everything, but not a single story. Do you want your life to be a collage of images and superficial experiences, or a story with depth and meaning? To give up something that you enjoy just because you imagine that you will enjoy something else more is trading experience for fantasy. If you face these issues, you might have a lot more practice at making dreams than achieving results. Don't forget to practice getting results every once in a while, too.

Being is the antidote for confusion. Don't be confused about the past, because it's over. Don't be confused about the future, because that preoccupation will only distract you when the time does come for action. Let go of all the daydreams and thoughts that are busy with nothing and, instead, focus on sharpening your awareness of what is going on within you and around you. Then when the time comes for action, you will know what to do.

Do you ever feel lonely? Why is that? It probably has less to do with missing the company of others and more to do with wanting to avoid being alone with your thoughts. Being in the present moment assuages this discomfort by putting your ideas about what happened in the past and your fears about the future into perspective. They are only your own constructs and fantasies. They have little to do with the way things were, will be, and most important, are right now. And right now is the only time you can do anything about. Your understanding of past and future consists of only ideas, constructs. Any action or realization must always occur in the present moment.

A thirsty man will drink at the first opportunity. He does not wonder if his thirst is only his imagination, or if the water is a mirage. He does not come to a spring and suddenly decide to wait to drink until he has another opportunity to find water. He will not wander away regretting his hesitation and fantasizing about the next time he has the opportunity to drink. Keep in mind, if you are to achieve the realization of wisdom, the only place you may realize it is in the present moment. Like anything else, enlightenment always occurs *now*.

Being in the present moment will eradicate ignorance that stems from our misconception that the past and future are anything but our own constructs. Indecision, confusion, distraction, and overexcitement stem from this fallacy because they are symptoms of being held hostage by your mind in the past or future instead of being free to experience life. Abandon your delusion about time being fractured into tenses and here, in the present, you will see that there remains only the clear mind that perceives wisdom.

THE ESSENCE OF BEING

*"A seeker who relies on thoughts to practice
concentration is like a person trying to pour
nectar in a vase filled with sand. Only when he
removes the sand will he find room for the nectar."*

- **The Perfection of Being**   We exist in the present moment every moment.
- **The Backdoor Approach**
  Step Six: ALLOW yourself to be in the present moment.
- **Exercise**   When you feel overwhelmed, repeat your intention like a mantra until you feel calm, and then analyze your situation.
- **Benefits**   Realizing the perfection of being solves problems with ignorance such as
  - scattered thoughts, ADD
  - obsession with thrill seeking
  - not finishing what you start
  - guilt
  - regret
- **Conclusion**   In order to perceive wisdom, you must live in the present moment.

Unity itself and the idea of Unity are already two.

—THE BUDDHA

Otto and Hannah crouched on the floor in the strange room off the foyer, with their backs pressed against the door. On the other side they could hear Emma Wycombe creeping across the foyer. Then light flooded in at them through the crack under the door, and they could hear Emma mumble something that sounded threatening in Chinese.

Otto and Hannah looked at each other, confused. Emma mumbled very quickly to herself in that foreign tongue and then stopped abruptly.

Her footsteps approached their door and she paused. Neither Otto nor Hannah dared breathe. Then Emma took a few steps away. They heard the cranking of gears, the rattle of the glass clock cabinet closing, and then the reassuring ticktock, ticktock of the clock in the hall resumed after its three-minute respite. Then the lights went off in the hall and they heard Emma climb the stairs back to bed.

Hannah and Otto relaxed enough to note their

surroundings. With the dark wood paneling, glass book-cases, and the majestically carved desk, it was obvious they were in Drake's personal study. A perfect miniature of an Asian temple was built into one whole wall. The model was complete with a tiny reflecting pond and bon-sai tree landscaping glowing under purple grow lights built into the sky over the temple. The detail was stunning.

"Okay," Hannah said to Otto, tearing her eyes away from the glorious shadow box. "Emma's gone. Let's go. Let's just make a break for it and run out the front door."

"Make a break for it? Who talks like that?" Otto said in a hushed voice. "Anyway, no one's breaking anything, Hannah. Didn't you see the lock on the front door? One of those two-sided locks. And we don't have the key."

"That's a fire hazard!" Hannah whispered.

"Really? Why don't you go wake up the Wycombes and tell them. I'm sure they'd want to know that. We *could* have just ducked back in the trapdoor, but you locked us out!" Otto said, his voice rising as much as he dared let it.

"I got the panel, didn't I?" Hannah held it up to prove her point.

"Well, let's have a look then."

"Here?" Hannah asked.

"You'd prefer to read it in the kitchen over a cup of tea?"

"I don't know what that Chloe girl sees in you," Hannah said, unwrapping the panel as quietly as possible.

"Fancy that, a bonus panel!" Otto said.

Sure enough, inside the wrapping were two black panels. At the center of each was the image of a pair of golden fish. They read the translation together in silence:

"A seeker who relies on knowledge to practice wisdom is like someone who attempts to catalogue and know each grain of sand; his subject is overwhelming. If he does not rely on knowledge to practice wisdom, he can see perfection within himself and each grain of sand:

both are impermanent,
free from conceptualizations,
physically interdependent,
under one another's influence,
and both exist, but not as separate phenomena.

The seeker and each grain of sand in the universe are one. To realize enlightenment one must recognize that true wisdom is understanding unity."

"Okay, let's come back to that," Otto said. "Now, where's my clue?" To his relief, on the next page were the words he sought.

"If you meet the Buddha on the road, turn him away. Give up the idea that enlightenment can be found anywhere outside of yourself because nothing is outside of yourself. To be

truly liberated, you must realize that even the many num-
bered things of the earth are not separate as they appear,
but united in one system. When you can realize this, you
will find the key that unlocks the backdoor to enlighten-
ment."

"I thought the saying was, 'If you meet the Buddha on the road, kill him.' I thought we were supposed to kill him," Hannah said.

"Yeah, trample his mandala, dismantle his priceless books, vandalize his waterfall, break into his house, and kill him. That's you watching too much American television. I, for one, am happy we don't have to kill anyone to read further in our little black book. But Annie Oakley here's on a crime spree," Otto said.

"I was just saying that maybe there's a hint there. *Turn him away.*"

"Well, I'll keep that in mind if we ever make it out of here back outside." He followed her eyes to the master-piece temple of pearl, jade, and gold before them. "Oh, no you don't."

She walked over and peered through the open golden temple doors. Inside all of the walls were intricately painted with elaborate scenes and carved relief. On the temple's floor was a miniature sand mandala just like the one Otto had destroyed, surrounded by miniature maroon cushions. There was a long golden horn and a drum that would have been enormous had it been life-sized. There were also many statues inside, adorned with tiny white scarves and minuscule flower garlands, but against the back wall of the temple Hannah saw what she was looking for.

"There's a little Buddha statue in there," she said. Otto glanced in to confirm this fact. Sure enough, inside there was a little statue of a standing Buddha, about seven inches tall. Otto shook his head trying to keep what she was saying out.

"There is absolutely no indication that we are supposed to touch anything in this room. How could Drake even know that we would end up here?"

"How could he have known a lot of things?" Hannah insisted.

"If we can't find a way out of here before morning, do you want to face the Wycombes sitting next to another priceless treasure that we've mangled?"

"I'm not going to mangle it," Hannah said. "I am just going to slip my hand in there and turn that statue."

"I absolutely forbid you to do this," Otto said as Hannah did exactly as she announced she would. Trying not to let her arm crush the interior of the temple, she attempted to rotate the golden statue. So far, so good. But the statue was stuck.

"It's fixed to the floor," she said.

"You are going to break it," Otto insisted.

She gathered up her courage and twisted the statue. A small wooden panel popped open in the temple roof.

"You've got to be joking," Otto said.

Inside was a numbered keypad.

" 'You must realize that even the perfectly numbered things of the earth are not separate as they appear, but united in one system,' " Otto read aloud from the translation. "Numbers. Not separate. Six Perfections, six numbers. Some of the clues had numbers. The first one was thirty-three. Page thirty-three, cabinet thirty-three. You wanna try that?"

"Don't you think we're rushing into this? We don't even know what that touchpad does. With our luck, it will set off a bomb," Hannah said.

"Come on. Thirty-three. I'm feeling lucky."

"Be my guest," Hannah said, stepping aside.

Otto raised his hand to the keypad. Hannah bit her lip.

"Hold on," he said. "That clue wasn't a perfection. The first perfection was impermanence. The mandala. What was the call number for the case?"

"Forty-five," Hannah said without hesitation.

"Here goes." Otto typed in forty-five and a piece of the wood paneling in the wall adjacent to the temple creaked open about a half an inch. Hannah tried to shine her flashlight to get a peek at what was inside. There were stairs leading down, and she wasn't able to make out what was at the bottom of them. To open the wood paneling further, it was clear they'd have to enter another number.

"The bodhi leaf had an eight painted on the back of it,"

Otto offered. Hannah nodded, and he keyed in eight. The wood paneling opened another fraction of an inch.

"We had to light the third lantern," Hannah said. "Three."

Otto keyed in the number three. The paneling popped open, finally wide enough so they could see in past the bottom of the stairs. Hannah shined her flashlight in. "It's a vault, Otto."

"Do you see another panel? Or a key?"

"It's full," she said.

"Full of what?"

"Full of everything. Books, paintings," she strained to make out details. "It's like a dragons' plunder in there. Put in the next number."

"Twenty-two b," Hannah said. "The plaque on the basement door."

Otto keyed in twenty-two and the paneling opened further.

"Um, what was next?"

"The perfection of being," she said.

"I know, but I don't remember any number."

Hannah grasped her head in her hands as if to squeeze out an answer. "Basement, vase, soccer game, clock," she listed, trying to trigger the memory of a number.

"We're in the house, what about the address?" Otto offered. "If the basement was twenty-two b, upstairs must be twenty-two a. Fifty-five was the number on the door."

"Good point," Hannah said. "Try twenty-two again."

Otto pressed 22 and the wood panel instantly slammed shut. A soft buzzer sounded and continued in an unbroken call of alarm, getting increasingly louder as the seconds ticked on. Otto looked at Hannah, knowing the cause of their bad luck: she hadn't worn red. The curse of the Fu dogs. The alarm was getting louder. They were running out of time. "Time!" Otto thought.

Hannah ran over and locked the door while Otto struggled to punch in the numbers again: 33-45-8-3-12 for the big number at the top of the clock, and finally the last number—for the perfection of unity—the number 1.

The vault door clicked open. Otto closed the keyboard panel in the temple roof, and they both darted inside the vault. On the other side of the vault was a keypad just like the one on the outside. Otto now knew the combination so he closed the door behind them.

Once inside, Hannah felt around for a light switch and turned it on. She was right; they were surrounded by amazing treasures. Ancient books, scrolls, paintings, statuary, Greek ceramics, and jeweled cups surrounded them. Otto even caught a glimpse of a golden saddle. They were dumbstruck. Hannah picked up a copy of the Gutenberg Bible and waved it at Otto.

"Now do you believe me?" Hannah asked. "Now that you're standing in the Wycombes' vault filled with all the things that should be in the library's vault, now do you believe me? Do you believe they were stealing these things to fund the library? It doesn't look like it, does it?"

Otto looked around. It was hard to argue standing knee-deep in evidence. He nodded.

"What can we do about it, though?"

"Oh, I can do plenty," Hannah said. "But first let's find the key to the backdoor that Drake talked about in the clue."

They spent hours digging through the treasures in the seemingly endless vault, looking for the key, sometimes pausing to read a few pages from a rare book, sometimes lingering over the master brushstrokes in a priceless painting. While Hannah searched on for the key, Otto revisited the translation of the last panel they had found, finally understanding its meaning.

> *"If he does not rely on knowledge to practice wisdom, he can see perfection within himself and each grain of sand:*
>
> *both are impermanent,*
> *free from conceptualizations,*
> *physically interdependent,*
> *under one another's influence,*
> *and both exist, but not as separate phenomena.*
> *The seeker and each grain of sand in the universe are one.*
> *To realize enlightenment, one must recognize that true wisdom is unity."*

Otto looked up and caught his own image in an old mirror propped up at the back of the vault and thought about those words. His image looked more tired than he felt, and on closer inspection he saw the tiny changes, his breathing, blinking, the vein throbbing in his neck, that demonstrated how ever changing and impermanent he was. Was he this body that he saw before him? He had to be more than this fleeting shell that would die and decay.

Then he had to laugh a little out loud. When dogs look in the mirror they bark, thinking there's another dog staring back at them. His idea of himself was not much more advanced than that. He was not this image he saw in the mirror, his idea of himself, or anyone else's idea of him. He was free to accept or deny his ideas about himself and any emotions these ideas would bring about. Therefore they could not be who he really was.

He reached out and touched that other self in the mirror. Just glass. And as the mirror moved from his touch, his image wavered in front of him, and then bumped back into his finger. Where did he end and the mirror begin? Physically he knew that the atoms between them did not create a clear boundary but blended together. His actions bound him to his surroundings by the effect he had on them and them on him. And his intentions affected them.

He and the mirror both existed, but not the way he had thought when he initially examined himself there. Now the boundaries between himself and the mirror, the vault, Hannah, broke down. And he saw how they did not exist on their own but were intricately tied together and to the rest of the world, with his unborn child, with the universe. In that moment, he saw the perfection of unity.

"I got it," Hannah said.

Otto shook himself from his thoughts. The world appeared different now, as if he and his surroundings were floating in the same ocean, subject to the same gentle waves. And he realized that on some level he was also causing the waves.

"What?" he asked.

"Are you okay?" Hannah said when she saw Otto. He looked miles away.

"Yeah, I just realized what this panel means. This unity thing."

"Well, you don't have to worry about that anymore," Hannah said. "I found the key! We can go find the backdoor."

"Where did you get that?" Otto asked.

"In that cabinet over there. Come on, let's go back, punch in the code, and get out of here. What were the last two numbers?"

After being so relaxed and so deep in thought, Otto felt jarred by Hannah's sudden urgency, and a little disturbed.

"No," Otto said, and looked back at the mirror recapturing that feeling he had just experienced. He saw then that something was truly off with Hannah, something that had been there all along, but he had been unable to put his finger on it until now. He went over to the black lacquer cabinet where she said she had found the key. On the cabinet was stenciled a pair of golden fish.

"What are you doing? I said I already have the key. Let's go."

Otto looked inside. The cabinet was filled with rows of golden keys, just like Hannah's access key, hanging from hooks. They were all labeled—*front door, bathroom, main house, study, and classroom*. The one that said *backdoor/office* was missing.

"We had the key all along?" Otto asked.

"Yeah, isn't that wild. The key that Mrs. Granger gave us," Hannah said. She handed the key to Otto. He turned it over in his hand and looked at it closely.

"Did you see this?" he asked, showing Hannah. Stamped in the key ever so faintly, worn from years of use, was a lotus.

"Like from the nomad story. The lotus spring," he said.

"Cool. And I think it really might be to the backdoor of the library. That's where the last clue is. Don't you want to go get it?" Hannah asked.

"There's another key missing in here, Hannah. The vault key. I don't suppose you have that, too?" Otto said.

She paused for a moment and blushed heavily. "It wasn't there, I swear."

Otto saw right through her. "What are you going to do with it, Hannah?"

"I don't have it," Hannah insisted.

"Don't look at me like that. I want to know the truth, and I can wait in here forever."

"It's not what it looks like, Otto. The Wycombes are robbing the library blind. Look at all this stuff! I've been in contact with a curator of a very famous museum. They are willing to do almost anything to secure this stuff before the Wycombes steal it and sell it off to private collectors."

"Even steal it themselves, for the museum?" Otto spat back. "I can't believe the act you put on at the Derby, like you were offended I even mentioned selling it, when that was your intent all along."

"It's not like that. You said it yourself; Drake would have wanted his collection to be available to everyone. That could still happen if it went to a museum."

"You think they're going to just set stolen property out for the world to see? Think about it, Hannah. But I'm sure you did think of that, didn't you. What's in this for you? Money?"

"A job," Hannah admitted. "I'd be librarian over the museum's whole collection of books. Even these."

Otto shook his head. "I can't believe you'd be so daft as to imagine they'd hire you after all that. And why involve me?" Otto asked.

"Obviously, that was an accident. The night we found the first panels, my contact at the museum had just informed me of the offer. I was just trying to get the books put away and search for the panels in the morning, but then . . ."

"I think I remember the rest," Otto said, holding his hand up.

"Plus, you actually figured out the first clue. The panels weren't even part of the bargain, but—" Hannah caught herself.

"But now they are," Otto said. "You used me."

They both thought about the kiss at the bodhi tree but neither of them spoke about it, both for their own reasons.

Hannah's phone rang in her pocket. She looked at Otto.

"Get it," he said. "I don't care."

She looked at the caller ID and grew dizzy. "Hello."

Hannah listened for a moment and sank to her knees. She hung up without saying a word.

Her world had just grown dimmer. Before he even went into surgery, her father had died in his sleep. She couldn't believe it. She tried to think but her thoughts were interrupted by a rhythmic noise in the background. She realized it was the sound of her own voice repeating, "No, no, no, no."

Suddenly she felt like a trapped animal, unable to escape the truth. She would never see her father's smile again, never get the chance to think about him without this crushing feeling of loss ruining the memory. It wasn't possible that he could just suddenly be dead. She wasn't finished loving him; how could he be gone?

"You have to let me out of here," she said to Otto. "My father, he's . . ." She refused to say the word.

Otto grabbed her by the wrist and wrenched her to her feet.

"You little liar. You think I'm going to fall for that one again?"

"I swear," she said through her tears, "please. This is important."

"None of this has been important to you." Otto turned her around by her arm and held it pinned behind her. They stood now facing the mirror as she cried. "Look there and tell me what you see," he said and turned her head with his other hand to make sure she did. Tears streaked down her face. "Are you this amazingly selfish girl in the mirror? This thief and liar?"

"No," she sobbed. "They stole this stuff first. I was only helping!"

"Look! Are you this girl who's too afraid to be successful, and who'll never have a happy relationship because YOU CAN'T BE TRUSTED? If your father is dead, I hope he can see you now," Otto said, pressing her face against the mirror. "I'm sure he'd be right proud of you."

"Let me go!"

"I will let you go when you'll take a good look at yourself. Then you can take the panels, the key, and do whatever you want with them. It doesn't make one bit of difference what happens."

She looked into the mirror and utterly broke down. Otto let her go, and sat by the door while Hannah stood transfixed in front of the mirror.

This was not who she was, she decided. Not this girl, not these labels, not this body. Her actions were not hers alone but part of an endless line of actions and intentions tying her inextricably with the rest of the world. And now her intentions were to free herself from these terrible feelings and ideas. She took a jeweled cup from the floor and threw it, smashing the face in the mirror. As the mirror came crashing down, she was shocked and relieved to see her image fall away so easily. And she knew she'd never be its prisoner again.

Where the mirror once stood was now only a gilded frame. Behind that she saw a door that had been previously hidden.

She took the vault key out of her pocket and placed it in the lock. The door opened and Otto and Hannah found themselves standing in a small chamber with a few dusty books. Another door stood before them. She used her key again and they found themselves at the threshold of the philosophy library.

"How is this possible?" Hannah asked, wiping away her tears.

"Just two doors on either end of one vault," Otto said.

"But I saw the vault with my own eyes."

"You just didn't recognize that there was more to the vault than what you saw. So how could the Wycombes be stealing if the books have never left the library vault?"

Hannah took a moment to reorganize her ideas about the Wycombes, herself, and her relationship to the world. Suddenly she knew her father wasn't so far away at all. In every sense he was part of her and always would be. She would miss seeing him and laughing with him, but she was certain that the best parts of him were still alive in her. His ideas and the actions he had set into motion over the course of his life would continue until the end of time. He would never be gone.

She handed the vault key back to Otto. He returned it to the cabinet before finally closing the door on their search.

ILLUMINATING UNITY

The last obstacle to the backdoor to enlightenment is another form of ignorance: the ignorance of the fact that we are one with the rest of existence, working parts of one system. Everyone and everything is interdependent to the point that nothing can be definitively separated. We might grasp this intellectually, but we usually don't live our lives as though we believe it. We are accustomed to thinking about ourselves as one thing, and the world around us as something completely different. To experience the incredible benefits of fully realizing this truth, we need to further examine the world, ourselves, and the real relationship between them.

To begin with, we are in the habit of thinking about the world around us in two different ways, from the relative perspective and the ultimate perspective. These viewpoints produce two separate, but very valid truths about the world and our lives. *Relative truth* is knowledge, a collection of facts and trivia, details. Everyone has his or her own special collection. No two people share the same perspective, and thus, no two people share the same relative truth. Knowledge is relative for these reasons:

- **Appearances are relative.** Because we can never see any object from all angles, there will always be a discrepancy between our perception of an object and the way it actually exists.
- **Value is relative.** Few things can be considered to be in everyone's best interest; therefore, individuals' values vary.
- **Facts are relative.** As our understanding grows, we outgrow our facts. In extreme conditions, our notions about time and space break down, and many

things, such as speed or direction, can be determined only when compared to something else.

It can be fun to process knowledge. Sometimes
knowledge can be useful for survival and comfort; however, facts are infinite. The total body of human knowledge contains the perceptions and conclusions of every
sentient being who has ever lived and will ever live. That
collection of facts grows exponentially with every second
that passes. One human brain is not remotely capable of
processing such an enormous amount of information.
This relative truth, in its entirety, is unknowable by any
individual.

The *ultimate perspective*, or the truth about the nature
of things as they really exist, is even less knowable. This is
the truth beyond conceptualization and language. We are
used to thinking about constructs—a kind of mental
symbol or shorthand for the object as it ultimately exists.
To apprehend ultimate truth, we need to leave our constructs and conceptualizations behind, the way we must
leave our knives and guns behind when passing through
airport security. No language allowed beyond this point.
Our concepts are too limited to fully grasp the ultimate
nature of anything. Ultimate truth is, by definition, inde-
scribable.

We are in the habit of seeing the world from the
relative perspective—an infinite collection of nouns, ac-

tions, and trivia—though we know from an ultimate perspective—an unknowable mystery beyond our grasp— everything would appear much differently. It's no wonder we feel separate from it. But who is this person who feels separate? Who is this "I"?

On the relative level, what does our concept of "I" consist of? What is it exactly? Is it a one-person unit? Is this unit a body? Emotions? Is it our perceptions? Is it our actions? Our minds? Is it something more? We can answer "yes" to all of these things, but we know we are not any one of these elements, but rather all of them. What combination of these parts, in what ratio, are we? With so many variables involved, can we really consider ourselves a unit?

Are we permanent in any sense? We all know that we are born and we die, but as we change so much every day, growing and aging and carrying around different food in our stomachs, why do we still consider ourselves the same person from one moment to the next?

Our idea of "I" is remarkably elastic. This fact indicates that a physical body does not necessarily fix the boundaries of "I," but rather we model our concept of self after the example set by others. We also limit our notion of self on the cues offered to us by others. "I" is a learned belief and custom, like culture.

Children sometimes extend their identity to include their parents or their possessions, which is why toddlers will say "mine" so much. Eventually they grow up and notice where adults commonly draw the line and follow suit. Parents often consider their children as part of themselves, if even on a subconscious level, until the child begins asserting his or her own boundaries, usually at age two. This can be a time of great trial for parents who might feel "betrayed" by the child, and they might eventually exclude the child in their idea of self.

"I" also extends beyond physical boundaries when we identify with political, religious, and national groups. Since we choose these identities, it is entirely possible to change them.

So what are the boundaries of your self? We realize the perfection of being, so we know that we exist, but how do we exist? When you think of "I," what is it that you refer to? Where does the "I" start and where does it stop? Are the boundaries your skin? When did the "I" begin and when does it end? Does the "I" start when you are born and end when you die?

We each appear independent from everyone else, a permanent, indivisible person. But are you independent? You may earn your own living, have your own thoughts, but you are only here because your parents created you. Your existence depended upon them. You are dependent upon others who bring your food to your table; you depend on the earth and the atmosphere; you are even dependent upon your own parts. You are the result of causes and you create causes. You are an effect, and you affect others.

Everything we see and perceive, the observable universe, is part of a single system. Living within that system affects us so profoundly that we are who and what we are precisely because of our dependence upon it. That system, our universe, is what it is because of its dependence upon us and all the rest of its constituents, much as a liver is not the progeny of an abdomen but a living part of a whole body. The system nourishes it, disposes of its waste cells, shelters it from the elements, and protects it from disease. The liver does not act alone, but in tandem with the rest of a body. You would be a very different person without your liver, and your liver would be a very different little hunk of flesh without you.

In turn, we depend on the earth for our existence. Our breath connects us to the atmosphere, a mixture of gases surrounding the planet. We breathe in and out, and oxygen courses through our arteries. Not only our feet, but also our digestive system connects us to the ground, or the lithosphere. We continually take in and expel minerals that come from the soil, much like an earthworm on stilts. We are connected to the life cycle in the earth's biosphere by our breath and digestive systems, as well. Plants transform carbon dioxide into the oxygen that we breathe. Other life forms, such as plants and animals, make up the bulk of the nutrients that we require for our food. We are connected to the waters of the earth in the most dramatic way, as approximately 72 percent of the human body's fat-free mass is made of water. We are part of the water cycle in our hydrosphere; when moisture is sucked out of the air, it is also sucked out of us. When the air around us becomes more humid, our skin soaks it up like the trees and soil.

We are connected to each other by the way we are generated, educated, and the way we help provide one another with the things we need for our comfort and survival. The decisions each of us makes and the actions we take affect us all.

The earth depends on its unity with the solar system. If you removed the earth from the system, that system would alter radically. The qualities of the other planets are what they are because the earth is in orbit where it is and how it is. Likewise, if the earth was the only planet spinning around the sun, there wouldn't be life on earth the way we know it, or possibly at all. The other planets aside, we are obviously also dependent upon the sun. Without the sun, life would not exist. Without the earth, the sun would be burning at a different rate.

Our solar system depends on our universe, and so on. And it works in the reverse, too. When something even as tiny as an atom is altered—like when human beings split an atom—it causes tremendous amounts of energy to be released, potentially creating great destruction. We then become immediately aware that the atomic system is part of our system by the extreme effects we experience.

Not only do we rely upon our own personal system of our bodies, but we also rely upon the systems within us and the systems we are within. If they affect us, we are not independent of them. Their existence and ours are entangled to such a degree that it would be impossible to separate them without radically altering everything involved.

Further, it is not even possible to completely remove any part of a system from the sphere of its influence. We can excise an offending organ from our bodies, but it will still decompose within our world. Its decomposition will have countless effects upon our planet.

Where does this great system of entangled systems end? Follow it out with your mind for a moment. What border can you imagine that doesn't rub up against another? There is no beginning and no end. We can shuffle things around and change their states, but we can't get rid of them. We are all in this one thing together. The whole of it is our true body.

We usually think of ourselves as existing outright, but our existence is "empty" of any independent factors. That is what Otto and Hannah realized when they looked in the mirror. Every part of your existence depends on something else. Once we can see the empty nature of our own highly prized selves, like Otto and Hannah did, we will be able to see it in the world.

Understanding this idea of "emptiness" is critical to realizing enlightenment. But as important as this is, spiritual teachers rarely approach the subject directly. They either offer an endless list of prerequisites for the student to perform before he or she is given the definition of emptiness, or they couch the idea of emptiness in mysteries, ambiguities, and magic. Thus the road to enlightenment is just as obscured as the destination. The Indian philosopher Nagarjuna clearly defined emptiness in the first century A.D. Phenomena are empty because they are

1. impermanent
2. thought of as separate
3. dependent on other phenomena for their beginnings
4. rely on one another for their course of action
5. exist, and are
6. Unified (because they are all empty of any independence)

If we examine the perfections we have covered in the previous chapters, we see that we already understand these qualities of emptiness:

- **Impermanence:** Our world is ever changing.
- **Freedom:** We are free from the prison of our constructs that appear to compartmentalize the world.
- **Causality:** Phenomena are created through the cycle of cause and effect.

- **Intent:** Phenomena are influenced by our intentions.
- **Being:** We exist.
- **Unity:** We are one with the rest of existence.

Now, we only need to see those qualities of emptiness in all things. As we determine the emptiness of each individual thing, it leads us back to recognize the unity that encompasses everything. We automatically understand that while a precious book from the vault might appear permanent, there once was a time when it did not exist and there will be a time when it will disintegrate. We see that while a key seems to exist on its own, it depends on the key factory and the folks who work there. We see that though we have a word and a concept of a library, that the idea in our mind and the word *library* are not the building filled with books; they are just a word or a thought. In fact, when we remove our ideas about how everything is unconnected, all we have left are objects that affect each other's existence so much that it is impossible to separate them. When we shatter the boundaries between ourselves, our ideas, and the world around us— much like Hannah shattered her own image in the mirror—we come to recognize the perfection of unity.

Understanding emptiness is the third perspective from which we can apprehend the world. It is the new frontier of our understanding. We are capable of comprehending and relating this *approaching perspective*, but it approximates the ultimate perspective as closely as our minds are able. The approaching perspective is the ground of enlightenment, the lookout point to the world as it really exists.

THE BACKDOOR APPROACH: UNITY

Recognizing the single theme that runs through all of existence will cure ignorance a whole lot faster than any collection of facts ever could. With this realization, any feelings of isolation you might have you can officially file under "unfounded." How could you be isolated when it is impossible to be disconnected from any system that affects you? When you realize emptiness and the perfection of unity, you can see that you are closer to your aspirations than you ever imagined.

> Step Seven: RECOGNIZE that you are already one with your goal.

Go out and get a taste of your goal. If there's a person you'd like to get to know better, go and make that first contact. Go and take a tour of your dream house if it's for sale. Test-drive your new car.

Imagine the person you will be when you have achieved your objective. How would he or she act? Dress? What would he or she say in conversation? What would you eat? How would that person spend leisure time?

Imagine all the qualities you would like to possess in detail.

Now do your best impression of that character. Start slow, maybe for an hour or two at a time. Build your wardrobe, your vocabulary. Transform the contents of your refrigerator. Even practice having the emotions and mental qualities you will possess when you have achieved your goal. There is not much difference between *acting* as if you're happy, confident, and charismatic and actually *being* happy, confident, and charismatic.

Eventually build your skill and stamina until you can play this character for days at a time, weeks, until finally not a trace of the unhappy, unsatisfied you will exist. Good riddance!

Usually it's better to eliminate the use of the possessive *my* from your vocabulary, to help limit your feelings of attachment, but that's not the case when focusing on bringing things into your life. If you are truly serious about materializing your objectives, develop the same feeling of possession and satisfaction of ownership that you feel about your own hand. Feel free to call the house down the street "my house." Call the person you would like to have a better romantic relationship with "my love." Don't be afraid to verbally own your goals.

You should not reinforce such feelings as desire, longing, or craving in relation to your goal as this simply creates more barriers and feelings of isolation. Only allow yourself positive feelings when thinking about your goal, and think about it as an extension of yourself.

Also get creative! Make pictures and collages of you and your goal together—even use a computer to combine images. Get as high- or low-tech as you want, as artistic as you feel like. The important thing is that you and your goal are visible together in one image. Create the representation on paper that you'd like to see in reality. Even add your written intent as a caption.

Visualize: Make yourself comfortable and close your eyes. Begin by taking a deep breath. Relax your body and mind. Take a moment once again and examine the emptiness of your self. Be aware of your breathing and the constant movement of your body and the change in your thoughts. Feel the air and your clothing on your skin and your physical contact with your chair. Recognize how what happens around you alters your thoughts. Now notice how you imagine yourself and realize that this identity is only a construct. Now examine your objective. Does any aspect of it appear to change? Is it any more permanent than you are?

Picture all the ways you and your goal are interdependent. If your goal has any physical qualities, imagine all the ways you are linked together. Imagine connections to the people who created it, worked on it, or maintain it, connections to the materials used, resources such as water, earth, and air that connect you. If your goal relies on your own nonphysical qualities, see how those qualities are simply unexpressed aspects of yourself.

Next, see how your ideas separate you from your aim. Melt these ideas away until you can see you and your goal merge as one.

BENEFITS

Understanding unity helps to solve humanity's biggest challenges. There is no such thing as an isolated problem. By injuring any part of the world's system, you injure yourself. There is no such thing as a win/lose situation. Think of life on this planet in terms of systems and not detached elements. Broaden your field of vision and assimilate the knowledge you have. See that the environment does not belong to any single country to exploit and then disregard. You cannot afford to think of your relationship with the earth as a one-night stand. There's no such thing as a free glass of milk. It's time to buy the cow.

When you understand unity, you will see that disease and starvation in other parts of the world affect you. Even if you don't mind seeing other people suffer, you will mind when their desperation becomes so great that they take their suffering to your doorstep and make it your own. Understanding unity cures this myopia. You will recognize that when two parts of the same system clash, that system will not perform optimally—and ultimately that system could fail. When you see all life as an extension of your own, you have realized the perfection of unity.

Living with the perfection of unity is recognizing that where there is a sacred spring in the desert, you are the desert and you are the spring. When you see that you are a sacred spring and the crowds gather to bow down before it, you are those worshipers. When those worshipers construct barriers to keep themselves from the spring, you are those barriers. And when a nomad returns from a long absence and walks beyond those barriers to drink freely from the spring, you are that man.

THE ESSENCE OF UNITY

"The seeker and each grain of sand in the universe are one."

- **The Perfection of Unity** You are one with the rest of existence. Everything is interdependent to the point that it cannot be separated.
- **The Backdoor Approach**
  Step Seven: RECOGNIZE that you are already one with your goal.
- **Exercise** Examine the emptiness of yourself and your goal. See how you are already one with it.
- **Benefits** Realizing the perfection of unity solves problems stemming from ignorance such as
  - feelings of isolation
  - environmental issues
  - war
- **Conclusion** You were already living enlightenment, now you understand it. The extent to which you choose to recognize emptiness in your life is up to you.

All truths are easy to understand once they are
discovered; the point is to discover them.

—GALILEO GALILEI

It was more than a week before Hannah returned to the library, carrying *The Backdoor to Enlightenment* panels carefully rewrapped and stacked in her book bag. As she walked up the driveway, Otto came down his office stairs to meet her in the courtyard.

"You're still working weekends here?" she called out to him as they walked across the parking lot toward each other.

"Actually, no," he said. "I don't work here at all. Just packing up the rabbit hole. Gathering my meager possessions and pushing off."

"Wow. Congratulations," Hannah said.

"Yes, thank you. Went and got me a real job."

"As a . . . ? I'm curious to know what you think is a real job?"

"I'm a fish biologist, least that's what my schooling's for. This brilliant nose of mine comes in handy."

Hannah was amazed. "What do fish biologists do exactly?"

"Well, for starters, I'm catching a gig on one of those big commercial fishers out of Canada, testing the catch, the water, and so on. But I'm only signed on as far as Carlyle. Then I'll be working full-time for the Scottish National Trust. Preservation work mostly, maybe a few speeches at fancy dinners, that sort of thing," he said with a wink.

"You're going home?"

"Aye, and it's about time. I've got a whole life there waiting for me. And what about you?"

"I'm just here to drop these off," Hannah said. "I have to get back up the coast."

"Do you still have that gold key?" Otto asked slyly.

Hannah tensed up. "Don't worry, I'm giving it back."

"That's not exactly my point," Otto said, surveying the parking lot. Bookstore patrons and guests coming for a lecture milled around. Otto leaned in and lowered his voice. "You want to give it one last go?"

Hannah stepped back, unsure of his meaning.

"Not between you and me!" he said. "Your mind's always in the gutter. I've learned my lesson about you Yank girls. You want to try out that key? Find the last clue?"

Hannah thought about it a moment. She was happy to

have his trust and friendship back, but after all she'd been through, all the bad decisions she had made, she was reluctant.

"You know you want to finish this thing. Come on. This time, do it for yourself."

"Okay," Hannah said, feeling the familiar twinge of excitement. "Let's go."

They tried to look casual as they made their way through the courtyard, around the back of the library. Hannah tried the key on the gate. It didn't work.

"Then over we go," Otto said. He helped Hannah over the wall, tossed her purse to her, and then scrambled over himself.

They walked through the beautiful garden together. It looked different now after all they had experienced and learned. The plan of the garden now looked very deliberate, the waterways flowing through it in an organized system. They finally felt the peace there that the landscape architect had intended when he created the garden, and they appreciated the fine details of his work of art. They now appreciated things—like the texture of the soft ferns against the rocks and the careful grouping of the stones—they had previously overlooked. The trees in the distance didn't just appear smaller because they were far away; they actually were miniature trees—creating the illusion that the garden was much larger than it was. It was all remarkable. They noticed the white lilies blooming on the pond and knew they were finally about to realize their goal.

From the bodhi tree, a beautiful yellow bird watched them walk by. In the week that had passed, the turtle had nearly made it a quarter of the way home, up the hill to the waterfalls' upper basin.

They finally reached the outside of the secret door they had found hidden in the library's bookcase. Hannah handed Otto the key.

"Cheers, Hannah," Otto said.

"Don't mention it. If anything blows up or falls apart, it'll be your fault."

"You haven't changed one bit," Otto said to her and then smiled. "Believe it or not, that's a good thing."

Otto put the golden key into the backdoor lock and turned.

Or he *tried* to turn it. It didn't budge.

"Maybe they got the place rekeyed," Hannah said.

"Or we have the wrong key," Otto added.

"It worked on the other side!" Hannah insisted.

"Well, it sure doesn't open the backdoor now," Otto said with some frustration.

"You looking for the backdoor?" A rotund middle-aged man with a large shade hat tied around his neck and dusty work clothes approached.

"Are you the gardener?" Hannah asked.

"I am," the man said. "A job I'm honored to have. You must be Otto and Hannah."

"How do you know that?" Otto asked.

"Because I'm also the director here at the Philosophical Study Center."

"Robert Drake?" Hannah gasped.

The man laughed. "Certainly I don't look that old. Last I checked, the director was Henry Wycombe. That's me," he said, holding out his hand to be shaken in turn by Hannah and then Otto.

"I've been working here for years and I've never seen you," Otto said.

"I work mostly up at the house. I've got a nice little setup there where I can work on the books. I'm a numbers man. Emma's the one who loves to be around people. It's her passion really."

Otto and Hannah knew if they looked at each other, they'd laugh. Hannah wondered what Emma would be like to work for if she *didn't* like people.

"So that key's finally turned up?" Mr. Wycombe asked.

"Uh, yeah," Otto said, finally gathering the wherewithal to remove the key from the lock and surrender it to Mr. Wycombe's outstretched hand.

"It's been a while since I've seen this old thing," Mr. Wycombe said, examining it. "This is the key to the backdoor all right," he said, returning the key to Otto.

"It doesn't work," Hannah said.

"I suspect that's because this isn't the backdoor."

"It's not?" Otto asked.

Mr. Wycombe shook his head. "It was Drake who labeled the keys, and this door, here, was the door he used every day to come in and out of the library. This was his *front* door. The *back* door is the one that the public uses, the one off the courtyard."

"Well, that's right self-centered," Otto said.

"Ah, who isn't?" Wycombe replied. "You try your key in that door." He turned and began to walk away.

"Wait," Hannah called out. Mr. Wycombe turned back. "We found these in the library. I think it's an old Tibetan manuscript." Hannah produced the panels from her purse. "It's a pretty exciting find."

Mr. Wycombe dismissed her with a wave of his hand. "Put whatever it is in the upstairs office," Mr. Wycombe said without much interest. "And just leave the key under the mat. Mrs. Granger will be by at noon to open up the library."

Hannah nodded.

"Sorry you'll both be leaving us," he continued. "But I hear you have a job at a big magazine waiting for you," he said to Hannah. "And I understand you have a little one on the way," he said to Otto. Hannah had to look to Otto for confirmation. Even then she could hardly believe it. "In any event, I'm sure you will both do just fine out there in the world. I better get back to work on the garden," he said. "That wife of mine is a slave driver. You be sure to keep your chin up," he said, gave them a nod, and walked away.

Hannah and Otto clambered back over the wall.

"You didn't tell me you got a job at a big magazine," Otto said as they rushed through the courtyard to the library's *real* backdoor.

"Much like you didn't tell me your girlfriend is pregnant. I guess it's just been a day of revelations." Hannah turned to him and then smiled. "Congratulations, Otto."

"You too, Hannah."

They were ready to get down to business. Otto put the key in and turned. The lock clicked open.

They swung open the door and they found the library much in the same condition it had been since they both had been working there. No secret chamber revealed itself. No hidden book fell off a shelf. They stood on the threshold, a little disappointed.

"Come on," Hannah said, flipping on the light switch. "Take a last look around while I run these upstairs."

Hannah unlocked the office she never quite got around to making her own. It appeared as if the horrible Mrs. Granger had moved back in. Cards from the card catalog were stacked on the desk, and a thick tidy notebook lay open beside them. Hannah had to laugh when she read it. Mrs. Granger actually kept a log of who asked to see which books, and how many hours or minutes they kept them out of her control.

"Thank God I'm getting out before I end up like this,"

Hannah laughed to herself as she paged through the densely written, yet immaculate, notebook. Mrs. Granger's records went back for years.

Hannah took the panels from her book bag. It would be strange never to read the words again that had altered her life so profoundly. There wasn't a hint of regret for missed opportunities as she set the stack on the desk. She only felt as though she was letting go of some final burden, that now she was truly free.

She touched the handwritten words *"Backdoor to Enlightenment"* on that first package they had found, quietly thanking Drake for setting her on this quest.

Something caught her eye. Whether it was in the loops of the *b*s or the oversized *E*s, either way, the handwriting looked familiar. Her eye wandered back to the desk, to those neatly written cards, the nearly compulsive log. The handwriting was shakier than it had once been, but it was the same.

It appeared that Mrs. Granger not only knew about the panels; she had once translated them. Hannah shook her head. No wonder she was so attached to the place. She must have worked very closely with Drake. Was there always more to a person than met the eye?

"Find anything up there?" Otto said as Hannah descended the staircase.

"Nothing special," Hannah said. She was done telling Drake's secrets, even if they were also the horrible Mrs.

Granger's. "Just the inner workings of Mrs. Granger's mind."

"Ha!" Otto said. "That's a scary thought. Come here for a second."

Otto waited for her in front of the *School of Athens* replica.

"You're the expert, but does something look a bit off here? In the center?"

Hannah leaned in to study the picture. In the center Plato stood with his finger pointing up to the heavens as Aristotle pointed to the ground, each arguing his point, or were they? On closer examination, Hannah saw that Plato had his other arm on Aristotle's shoulder, and Aristotle looked back at him with a positive smirk on his face as if they were sharing the funniest joke in the world.

" 'Here's where the truth lies,' " Otto quoted Plato to Hannah beside him, " 'in the spiritual realm, in the unseen.' "

" 'Not a chance, old man,' " Hannah quoted Aristotle back at him. " 'The truth is right here on earth, in everyday things.' "

They both smiled. "Do you think they knew that they each had half of the truth? That the truth is in the seen and the unseen?" Hannah asked.

"That the truth lies in both the material world and the spiritual?" Otto said in a posh accent as if he were on a

BBC documentary. "You think these fellows read *The Backdoor to Enlightenment*?"

"By the looks on their faces, I wouldn't be surprised," Hannah said.

"Did Raphael put that in the original? Them all buddy-buddy?"

Hannah shook her head. "To tell you the truth, Otto, I don't remember."

Otto shrugged and Hannah turned off the lights.

As they left the Philosophical Study Center Library for the last time, locking the front door—which, from some perspectives, was really the backdoor—Otto grumbled.

"What?" Hannah said.

"It's just that it's cheap," Otto said. "It's just a key to the door?"

"Maybe it's a reference to all the books—how everything we see will seem different after reading the panels."

Hannah's life had done a complete turnaround since the night she had found the pages of *The Backdoor to Enlightenment*. The words that she had discovered had brought her closer than ever to her father, both in his last days and now that he had passed away. She was no longer afraid of who she was and what life held for her. As far as she was concerned, she lived in a whole new world.

"That's a rotten trick," Otto scowled. He was about to

insist that they had wasted all that time searching for a key to unlock a door that they entered every day, but he could not say the words. He knew it wasn't true. He wouldn't be signing on to do the work he enjoyed doing if he had never found the panels. He'd still be obsessed with drinking, and he wouldn't be getting on a boat to finally go home and start a new life with his son and—before too long, he hoped—his wife.

"Buck up, Otto. What'd Wycombe say?" Hannah reminded him. "Keep your chin up."

Instinctively, Otto and Hannah raised their eyes. There, above the door, was the sign they each had passed every day, some days reading it, some days choosing to ignore it, but now they saw that it meant more than they could have ever previously imagined: *Achieve what was never lost*. Above it was carved a single lotus.

ILLUMINATING ENLIGHTENMENT

What is enlightenment, really? It's more than just a happy feeling, right? It is an understanding that frees us from suffering. From our level, suffering looks like it breaks down into four parts, which we have already examined extensively: the suffering of pain and discontent, the suffering of constructs, the suffering of pervasive action, and ignorance. But in the most basic sense, suffering is just causality and our response to it. Pain could not exist without a cause or stimuli. Discontent could not exist without our minds reacting to the change around us. The suffering of pervasive action is only the result of being immersed in causality. Constructs and ignorance are just our minds again, reacting to causality. So, really, if we can take care of our own ignorance by realizing the Six Perfections, enlightenment only requires one little thing: freedom from pesky causality. So where are we going to find this noncausal land called Enlightenment?

Where, that is the key word.

How do we define "here" and "there"? *Here* is always where your concept of self resides. If you ask yourself, "Where am I?" You can always answer, "Over here!" Where is *there*? Anywhere *I* am *not*. So to use the words *here* and *there*, we must first buy into an idea of separateness and ignore the interdependence we now know we share with all other things.

If we are all part of a whole, we all share one "true body" that includes all space and time. We can't really *go* anywhere. Our true body cannot move beyond the space it occupies because we occupy *all* of space. We cannot exist beyond the duration our true body occupies because our true body includes all the time there is.

Take, for instance, the vault that Hannah and Otto explored. The Wycombes appeared to be stealing the library's treasures because their vault seemed to contain stolen treasures and the library vault looked as if it had been pillaged. But the truth was, these were not separate vaults at all, only two ends of the same room. No theft was committed—no action was taken—because books were not removed from one vault and brought to another. It is only when a person identifies two separate vaults that the illusion of a crime takes place.

This is the final quality of emptiness to recognize, thereby realizing enlightenment: There is no coming or going.

Precisely because of this unity, from the ultimate perspective, causality is actually not possible at all. Only the appearance of change exists. Our causality relies on time and space, and from an ultimate perspective, they aren't factors. We say that ultimate perspective is beyond conceptuality because our minds can't really grasp a reality without time or space. Can you imagine a world without here and there, or before and after? You might be able to imagine it in very abstract terms, but you won't be able to talk about it. We just don't have the words to describe that world.

Causality, as we know it, is much like the illusion of the world projected onto the world as it actually exists. This is the reality of limitless potentials unbound even by time and space. This liberation requires no striving, no attainment, and no realization. This is the realization of enlightenment. From the approaching perspective, we are already free of causality. From the relative perspective, we are its slaves. Which perspective will you identify with?

The perfection of enlightenment means that from the ultimate perspective, there is no action at all, only a wonderland of awareness in infinite combination, shining through itself, experiencing itself from every possible perspective. Every facet of our true body is unique. The purpose of relative truth is to know our true body completely. This is omniscience.

When we understand the emptiness of everything around us simultaneously as we see the separateness of the everyday world, that is the omniscience of enlightenment. We were already living it, now we understand it.

There's one more factor involved in enlightenment, which arises naturally from the realization of unity, and that is compassion. Once we understand that we are each connected to the rest of the world, we begin to view everyone's best interests as being as important as our own. We won't want anyone else to suffer any more than we want to suffer ourselves. If any part of the whole suffers, so will each of its pieces. As the level of unnecessary suffering in the world creeps up, our personal happiness will be negatively affected, and that is no fun.

This might seem like a wildly selfish attitude, but when viewing the world from an approaching perspective, we identify "self" with everything that appears to exist. This isn't personal compassion specifically granted and withheld on a case-by-case basis. It is rather limitless compassion without aim, encompassing the entirety of your true body: everything. Nothing and no one is excluded.

Usually when we think of compassion, we think about sympathy for the suffering of others, sometimes accompanied by a desire to help them. While often expressed with the best of intentions, this emotion, and the actions that stem from it, is capable of causing just as much harm as good. How often have you experienced an intrusion into your privacy and a violation of your freedom because someone else was determined to see that you received the "help" they thought you needed, whether or not you wanted it? Have you ever forced your will upon others in the name of caring and compassion? We all like to imagine that we have pure and unselfish motives, but everything we do, we do for a reason. We act compassionately toward others because we like to think that we are making other people happy, we enjoy the gratitude that results from our good deeds, we are avoiding feelings of guilt, or for some other reason. But can we honestly say that we act compassionately toward others because we are omniscient and we know what is in the best interest of everyone involved?

Usually we extend compassion only to people who appear to be suffering. We feel sorry for those in positions that we judge to be worse than our own, and we estimate that their positions would be improved with some assistance. When we see beings in positions we consider better than our own, we feel envy, awe, or scorn.

Imagine that there are two groups of people before you. One group is a homeless woman, ravaged by the elements, and her five young children. They all appear to be starving and dressed in rags. Some of the children are so weak from hunger that they cannot stand. In the mother's eyes, you see the torment of her helplessness to protect and care for her children. The other group is a group of young men dressed in expensive suits, laughing and having dinner at an upscale steak house. Which group of people do you feel more compassion for?

It is easy to feel sympathy and caring for people who are visibly suffering, but the truth is, all sentient beings are equally struggling. No one is any better off than anyone else. If the world of causality we see around us is like an ocean, the young businessmen are at the crest of a wave and the woman and her children at the trough, but both groups are wet. Their apparent fortune or misfortune is temporary, bound to change and reverse. Everyone gets old, gets sick, and dies. From the relative perspective, everyone suffers. Why then does it make more sense to us to extend kindness to some and withhold it from others? Are we so shortsighted?

The aimless compassion of an enlightened being is different. Enlightened beings recognize that all sentient beings suffer equally, though perhaps differently, on the relative level, and so they extend compassion to all, regardless of situation, without prejudice.

Aimless compassion is based on loving and caring. The fourteenth Dalai Lama once likened enlightened compassion to caring for the whole world as effortlessly as you care for yourself. He said that if you find you have a thorn in your foot, your hand would not pause and say, "I am not the foot; this is not my problem." Your hand would automatically reach down and remove the thorn. This seamless response is the attitude of universal responsibility that comes naturally to those with profound realization.

However, though the world appears to be struggling with the effects of causality, enlightened beings realize the unity behind the illusion of separateness. They know that on the ultimate level, there is no separate thorn or injured foot. Their aimless compassion then isn't based on sympathy for the suffering of others and a desire to help them; it is based on seeing the perfect nature of others and radiating the confidence that there is nothing in the world that needs to be fixed, but all must be loved. Ultimate reality cannot be threatened, but it can be embraced.

Enlightened compassion isn't pity. Pity is feeling sadness because of someone else's pain. This feeling is inappropriate for two reasons. First, reacting to other people's suffering by creating more suffering within you will not help anyone. By doing this you only add to the overall suffering in the world. Second, if you look at other people and imagine that they experience misfortune that you have been spared, you are deluding yourself. Human suffering comes in all shapes and sizes, but no one is spared; no one is special in this way.

When you realize the perfection of unity completely, you can eliminate all unnecessary suffering from your life, but you still get the struggling that comes from just living. You aren't going to eliminate pain, or the suffering associated with the changes of life. You will get old, hungry, sick, and then you will die. Humans have a range of probable experiences. Chances are, you'll get to experience the full gamut of them. There's no way around that. Not for you, not for the Buddha. Sorry. From the relative perspective, we all suffer and struggle; from the ultimate perspective, hardship is like an illusion. As you go through your life, you are free to identify with either perspective, or both. The choice is always yours.

Fostering universal responsibility is not a license to interfere with the lives of others, or impose your will upon them. This responsibility isn't based on action, but rather on correct identity—identifying with an ultimate rather than a relative perspective. It does not rely upon an individual's opinion of what it means to "help," but depends solely on the aimless compassion of harmlessness. This freedom from violence is the natural by-product of realizing the Six Perfections of existence.

A life is a whole made up of a collection of parts, perfections in their own right. Our perfection of impermanence is our form, or body. It is not meant to last, but it is built to grow, change, and die. Our perfection of freedom exists in our thoughts, able to be influenced, but free from the cause and effect that bind action. Our perfection of causality exists in our actions, reacting to stimuli and helping us to steer through the world. Our perfection of intent exists in this will to live, or in the life force that fuels actions. Our perfection of being exists in our consciousness, and the perfection of unity exists in our true body, all of existence. The perfection of our enlightenment is the integration of all of these, all perspectives and every perfection.

THE BACKDOOR APPROACH: ENLIGHTENMENT

Since you picked up this book, you've been involved in a lot of planning, thinking, and action. You've explored ideas that you might not have previously considered. It is to be hoped that you've had some fun along the way and realized a few of your dreams, but all in all, whether you realized it or not, you've been doing a lot of work. Now it's time to put down books and theories and start living!

Step Eight: LIVE your dream!

Visualize: Make yourself comfortable and close your eyes. Breathe deeply and relax your body and mind. Imagine yourself in your favorite place, wearing your most comfortable clothes. Are you indoors or outdoors? What is the weather or temperature like on this most perfect day? What do you see in front of you? What do you hear? What smells surround you?

Now think about what you'd most like to experience. Don't exclude even the impossible, for here in your enlightened mind all things are open to you. Have you always harbored a desire to fly like a bird? To explore outer space? Make a winning touchdown or goal? Take some time and explore your wildest desires. You are free to do whatever it is you want to do.

Now think of the goals you are accomplishing. Vividly imagine every detail of experiencing them. What you will be wearing, your surroundings, who will be there with you and what you will be doing. How do you feel now that you have achieved your final aim? Imagine the joy, excitement, and sense of satisfaction associated with obtaining your dream. Feel a smile spread across your face. Experience the joy until your face hurts from smiling. Now relax just a little bit. Okay, now open your eyes.

In your day-to-day life, the Six Perfections will guide you through nearly any obstacle you encounter. Say, for instance, that you are thirsty and find yourself near a deep well full of water. Conveniently, there is a bucket and a pulley and a rope all set up for you. All you need to do is pull on the rope and hoist the bucket full of water up from the depths of the well. Not too tricky. You pull and pull and with every effort the bucket moves steadily up the well closer and closer to your dry lips. The bucket is in sight, maybe a foot or two out of reach. But suddenly no matter how hard you pull, you are unable to hoist the bucket any closer. You have a problem.

If you have not realized the perfection of causality, chances are you will get frustrated. Being so thirsty yet unable to reach the water, you may violently yank on the rope until the rope breaks and the bucket tumbles down the well, out of your reach. If you have realized the perfection of causality, you will understand that something is causing the bucket to get stuck and you will look for the cause of the obstacle. Upon close examination you find that there is a big knot in the rope, and the rope is unable to pass through the pulley.

If you have not realized the perfection of courage, you will get discouraged, thinking, This pulley system doesn't work. The rope is unable to move any farther, and therefore I am unable to get to the bucket of water. Then you will go on your way and try to find some other source of water. If you have realized the perfection of courage, you will think, there is a real problem here, but I have a real need. Then with determination you will decide that you will give your best effort to resolve the problem.

If you have not realized the perfection of being, you will get distracted and won't be able to decide on one course of action. You will daydream about how great it will be when you get the water, think about your past failures and how you have never faced this problem before. You will get bored, regret that you ever decided to try this nonsense, and go and look for another well. If you have realized the perfection of being, you will remain focused on the real problem in front of you.

If you have not realized the perfection of unity, you will concentrate on gathering information about the parts, the rope, the pulley, and the bucket. You will focus on the details rather than the overall picture. When you have realized the perfection of unity, you will understand how the parts work together and how to get the water from the well to your mouth because you know that the overall picture includes you.

You will still probably get a drink even if you have not realized the perfection of enlightenment, but it will be a much richer experience if you have!

BENEFITS

Even if you aren't able to see the world from the approaching and relative perspectives in every moment of your life, there still is great value in experiencing the ultimate perspective once. Think of what our world would be like if all of humanity could at least sample enlightened realization. It would color everything we did thereafter. If you have tried chocolate cake, does it matter if you tried it for ten minutes or twenty-five? You know what it tastes like. Holding that understanding unshakably is enlightened realization.

Imagine a whole generation of children growing up with parents who choose to explore enlightened realization, even if it is only for a few moments here and there. If children grow up with enlightenment as a possibility instead of a myth, then their children will grow up perfecting it. You will be able to take your consciousness to places you have never even imagined, until finally, even the illusion of identifying with suffering will be a distant dream.

So, if you've been paying close attention, you will see that you have always been enlightened. The choice to realize it or not is yours. Welcome to life as an awakened being. Before enlightenment, paying bills, cooking dinner; after enlightenment, paying bills, cooking dinner. But now all your potential and the full extent of your influence are perfectly obvious to you. You have the power to affect the causal world for any purpose that you wish to pursue. You realize the apparent separateness, the approaching causal nature, and the ultimate unity in all things. You are awakened. So now what are you going to do?

THE ESSENCE OF ENLIGHTENMENT

"Achieve what was never lost."

- **Enlightenment** is a state beyond causality. That state is unity and you are there.
- **Aimless compassion** is harmlessness, based on seeing the perfect nature of others.
- **The Backdoor Approach**
    Step Eight: LIVE your dreams!
- **Exercise**   Helping people to help yourself.
- **Benefits**   Realizing enlightenment even for a moment has benefits such as
    - relieving feelings of sadness because of other people's pain, and
    - raising our awareness until we no longer identify with suffering.
- **Conclusion**   Life is a learning experience. You are awakened. Now what are you going to do with your life?

After Mr. Wycombe left Hannah and Otto, he returned to the garden's teahouse in time to grab the last banana muffin before Mrs. Granger could get it.

When she gave him a sour look, he reminded her that she had already had three.

"Leave her alone," Emma said, taking the muffin from his hand and giving it to Mrs. Granger. "You don't need it."

"What have I missed?" A familiar face from the library came out of the main house. He had aged considerably, but for those who knew him he was still recognizable from his portrait on the library wall. The blue eyes were unchanged. Removing his tweed hat, the old man had a seat at the table.

"Only that your wife has eaten all the muffins," Mr. Wycombe said.

"I have no control over the woman, obviously. After thirty years I can't even get her to take my name." He leaned over and kissed Mrs. Granger's head. "Good morning, darling."

She feigned annoyance and waved him away. "Stop it, Robert."

He took out the newspaper and immediately lost himself in it.

"Well, you all will be pleased to hear that Otto and Hannah are finally on their way," Mr. Wycombe said. "I just met them in the garden."

His remark was greeted by a wave of sighs and *finally*s from the women at the table. Robert Drake acknowledged the news by simply rustling his paper.

"That Otto has been here for years! I never thought he'd leave. Not too bright. Three librarians have come and gone since he's been here, and he never caught on. I had given up on him. If it wasn't for that girl, he would have been ruining my bulletins forever," Emma said.

Mrs. Granger shook her head. "No, no. The girl was just as thick. Without him, I don't think she would have found the first panel if it bit her in the——"

Robert Drake cleared his throat over his newspaper, silencing Mrs. Granger.

"I don't see how he even got involved. Probably some shady business. She mentioned something about an offer from a museum?"

Drake stole a glance to see if anyone was looking at him. No one was. What they didn't know wouldn't hurt them. Everyone needed an extra push once in a while, and if he had to pretend he was a museum curator to help, then so be it.

"Well, all's well that ends well," Mr. Wycombe said. "I've e-mailed the monks and they'll be here next week to begin working on the new sand mandala. Mrs. Granger, can you see to it that all the other panels are replaced? We have a new librarian starting on Monday."

Mrs. Granger nodded.

"I'm surprised you don't take more of an interest in these things, Robert. You're the one who started this whole business."

"He was a young man, then. Back when he thought he needed to save the world," Mrs. Granger said.

"Well, Emma and I are glad you did, Robert. We sure enjoyed your treasure hunt back in our day."

"Speak for yourself!" Emma said, but then lovingly squeezed her husband's hand under the table.

Robert Drake set his paper down. "It was my pleasure."

"Remember those days? That night we spent in the basement," Mr. Wycombe said to Emma. When he received no response, he turned to Robert. "I know you're not interested in our daily dramas, but I'm glad you let us share the manuscript like this. I think the kids get a lot out of it."

"I thought it might be fun if other people could discover the panels the way I did. I'm too into my studies to get involved now, but—"

"What do you mean, 'discover them like you did'? I

thought you bought those panels at a flea market?" Mrs. Granger said.

"I did," Drake said over his paper. "In Cairo."

"Cairo?" Emma and Mrs. Granger exclaimed simultaneously, both confused for different reasons.

"You told me you first read them in Mongolia," Emma insisted.

"Well yes, that's where I read the *first* one."

Mr. Wycombe interrupted him. "But didn't you meet your translator in Calcutta?"

"Yes, but she was kidnapped, you see."

"She?" They all asked at once.

"Ah, you'd have to ask the late Mr. Granger about that," Drake said.

Mrs. Granger choked on the last of the banana muffin, a little to the pleasure of Mr. Wycombe. "No, no," Drake clarified to calm her. "It was before your time, dear. Johnny Granger was always faithful. A good man. The very best." Mrs. Granger relaxed a bit before Drake slipped in, "Although she was the reason he lost his arm."

When he saw the confusion that his explanation had caused and the questions that still hung in the air, he set down his paper and took up his coat and hat.

"Where are you going, dear?" Mrs. Granger called after him.

"To the library to study. This is precisely why I retired," he said, shaking his finger at them.

He went into his study, shut the door, and pulled a map out of a compartment in the floor of the diorama.

To satisfy their questions would take hours, and he could see no point in dwelling on the past. He checked his watch and then dialed his cell phone. He was working on a new discovery that—as soon as he recovered the pertinent documents—would change the world.

He would need help, but he knew just the person

Somewhere across town, Otto sat in the back of a yellow cab heading for the airport. His cell phone vibrated in his pocket. He fumbled to get it out. Private number.

"Aye?"

"Otto Mackenzie? My name is Robert Drake. I have an errand I would like you to run for me."

"Who is this?" Otto demanded.

"I have located a treasure that I have waited my whole life to secure. And I'd like you to go find it for me. This errand would take you only a few weeks, at the end of which I will pay you double whatever they're paying you on that boat, and provide you with a first-class ticket home in time for the birth of your son."

"I'm listening," Otto said against his own better judgment.

"What if I told you that there was another stage of the path to enlightenment?" the voice on the other end asked him.

"There's more?" After all he had learned, what else

could there possibly be? Then Drake told him something he could not believe.

Otto looked at the phone in his hand. He tapped the cabdriver on the shoulder. "Could you, uh, stop the cab, sir?" As the cab pulled over to the curb, Otto put the phone to his ear again.

"I'm ready" was all there was left for Otto to say.

ZA RINPOCHE is a Tibetan monk who first came to the world's attention when his life story was chronicled in the first chapter of Po Bronson's megabestseller, *What Should I Do with My Life?* While growing up in a refugee camp in Southern India, he was recognized by the Dalai Lama as the sixth reincarnation of the Za Choeje Rinpoche. He is the founder of the Emaho Foundation, a nonprofit organization based in Scottsdale, Arizona, dedicated to sharing Tibetan culture with the West, supporting humanitarian projects, and assisting with personal spiritual development. Za Rinpoche teaches throughout the world, while maintaining his obligations as the spiritual leader to many monks.

ASHLEY NEBELSIECK is an author and adventurer. She studied art history and religious studies at Arizona State University, and travels all over the world checking out sacred sites—from the Vatican, to the pyramids at Giza, to Callenish in the Outer Hebrides, to Angkor Wat in Cambodia, and countless others. She currently lives and writes in Scottsdale, Arizona.